Training for Environmental Groups

J. Clarence Davies, Frances H. Irwin,
Barbara K. Rodes

The Conservation Foundation
Washington, D.C. 20036

Training for Environmental Groups

Cover design by Sally A. Janin
Typography by Rings-Leighton, Ltd., Washington, D.C.
Printed by BookCrafters, Chelsea, Michigan

The Conservation Foundation
1717 Massachusetts Avenue, N.W.
Washington, D.C. 20036

Library of Congress Cataloging in Publication Data
Davies, J. Clarence.
   Training for environmental groups.
   Includes index.
   1. Environmental policy—Societies, etc.—Employees—Training of—United States.   2. Environmental protection—Societies, etc.—Employees—Training of—United States. I. Irwin, Frances H. II. Rodes, Barbara K. III. Title.

HC110.E5D36   1984   363.7 '07 '0683   84-9443

ISBN 0-89164-083-5

Training for Environmental Groups

The Conservation Foundation is a nonprofit research and communications organization dedicated to encouraging human conduct to sustain and enrich life on earth. Since its founding in 1948, it has attempted to provide intellectual leadership in the cause of wise management of the earth's resources.

Contents

Foreword   ix

Acknowledgments   xi

Executive Summary   xiii

Chapter 1: Introduction   1

Diversity of Environmental Groups   1
Changing Conditions Mean New Training Needs   3
The Conservation Foundation Report   5
References   6

Chapter 2: Training Needs of Environmental Groups   7

Specific Training Needs   7
    Fund-raising and Membership Recruitment   8
    Internal Management   12
    Communications and Education   17
    Research and Policy Development   22
    Six Rankings of the 30 Surveyed Skills   23
Overall Priority of Training   25
    Overall Importance of Training   25
    Training Being Provided   33
    Willingness to Use Funds and Time for Training 36
    Attitudes toward New Institutions   37
Interviews with Representatives of Environmental Groups   38
References   42

116060

Training Provided by Environmental Groups   48
   Association of New Jersey Environmental Commissions   49
   The Land Trust Exchange   49
   New England Environmental Network   50
   Northern Rockies Action Group   51
   Sierra Club   52
   *League of Women Voters of the United States/League
     of Women Voters Education Fund*   53
   Summary   55

Training Provided by Other Organizations   56

   Traditional Institutions   56
    Publications   57
    American Society for Training and Development
     (ASTD)   57
    American Management Association (AMA)   58
    American Society of Association Executives (ASAE)   58
    National Training Laboratories (NTL), Institute for
     Applied Behavioral Science   59
    Universities   59
    Volunteer: National Center for Citizen Involvement   60
    United Way   60

   The Grantsmanship Center   60

   Management Support Organizations   61
    The Support Center   62
    The Youth Project   62
    Community Training and Development   62

   Community-Organizing Training Centers   64

Graduate Environmental Studies Programs as a
  Training Resource   66

   Environmental Studies Programs at a Crossroad   67

   *Profiles of Some Graduate Environmental Studies
    Programs*   68
    Duke   68
    UCLA   68
    University of Michigan   69

   Internships and Fellowships   70

*Environmental Studies Programs as Training Grounds
for Environmental Groups*   73

Funding Sources for Training   74
   Government Support   74
   Industry Support   76
   Private Philanthropy   77

References   78

Chapter 4: Matching Needs, Resources, and Institutions   81

Needs and Resources   81

Linkage Between Needs and Resources   83

Coordinating Environmental Trainers   84

Policy Training   85

Graduate-level Environmental Studies   86

Internships and Fellowships   87

Management Training Program for Mid-Size Groups   88

Improving Management in the Larger Groups   88

Conclusion   89

References   90

Appendix A: Methodology and Sample   91

Appendix B: The Questionnaire   101

Appendix C: Training Needs by Individual Skill   113

Index   119

Foreword

In December 1982, The Conservation Foundation was asked by the trustees of the Richard King Mellon Foundation to undertake a study of the training needs of environmental and conservation groups. We were also asked to examine whether any new institutions were needed to provide such training. This report contains the findings and conclusions of our research.

In the course of conducting interviews for this study, we were struck by an anomalous discovery: some of the organizations with leaders who most acutely perceive the need for training do not budget for it. They know training is needed and that it deserves a priority. But several say they cannot afford it, or cannot afford as much as they need, or cannot afford to search out and systematically use sources of training.

More than one environmental group leader pointed to the way in which funding is provided as an important reason for the failure to offer training. Foundation funding for restricted projects often explicitly excludes the use of any such funds for overhead. Thus, no portion of such funds can be used for staff training, which is but one of the elements of overhead, along with rent, heat, library costs, and communication. Why not then approach a foundation for a specific grant for training? Such a grant would possibly replace a foundation's support of other, more costly project work in a given year, we were told. Then why not use unrestricted funds to fund training? The answer we heard so often: there is too little unrestricted support available. Many foundations, for example, provide little or no unrestricted support.

It is conceivable that the wariness of some foundations to make no-strings gifts to environmental groups, and the preference of foundations to provide funds only for specific projects, derives from a negative assessment of the overall management skills of many non-profit organizations. Interestingly, this negative assessment was shared by more than a few of the environmental organization executives we interviewed. If that is the case, funding institutions should know that the leaders of many grantee groups believe training in management skills could be very helpful. A vicious cycle emerges: inadequate funds for training fuels poor management performance, and poor management curtails raising needed funds, which could in turn be used to train and improve management.

So, the need for training exists. And, in general, the institutions to fulfill that need exist. The unmet need is to connect environmental users and providers of training. Our report thus recommends some steps that might be taken to match needs, resources, and institutions. A clearinghouse on environmental needs and resources, for example, seems indispensable, as is better training in substantive policy issues.

We hope that this report will serve as a basic resource and will stimulate further thought among environmental groups, trainers, government officials, academics, foundations, and the business community. Our report represents a first effort to deal with an important area of concern to environmental groups. We thank the Richard King Mellon Foundation for supporting it.

William K. Reilly
President
The Conservation Foundation

Acknowledgments

The authors are grateful to many people who helped with this report. The consultant on survey design was Robert Mitchell. The draft report was circulated widely for comment. The following reviewers deserve particular thanks: Nancy Anderson, Candace Ashmun, Joyce Bader, William Bryan, Judy Campbell Bird, Marty Fluharty, Robert LeDuc, Clarke Maylone, Marsha Ramsay, Mike Schechtman, Bob Segal, Isabelle Weber, Seward Weber, and Belinda Wilson.

Conservation Foundation staff who contributed energy and skill to this project include Jenny Billet, Gwen Harley, and Tony Brown; they coordinated lists and typed the manuscript. Bill Carroll reviewed all the tables for accuracy. And Bethany Brown and Bob McCoy ably edited the final report.

Executive Summary

Background

In response to a request from the Richard King Mellon Foundation, The Conservation Foundation examined the training needs of environmental and conservation organizations. This study, undertaken during 1983, analyzes environmental groups' perceptions of their training needs and describes the resources available to meet them. Changing political and economic conditions resulting in cutbacks in programs and regulations, the termination of government-funded citizen participation training programs, and the changing understanding of such environmental problems as acid rain and hazardous waste, all necessitate the need to strengthen management, research, and policy capabilities of environmental and conservation groups.

Study Methods

The Conservation Foundation study involved four tasks. A comprehensive 11-page survey was sent to 411 representative environmental and conservation groups throughout the United States, and the results, 225 completed questionnaires, were analyzed. Project staff interviewed leaders of environmental groups, funding sources, and training providers. A small one-day conference was convened to discuss the future of graduate-level environmental studies programs. And a literature review was undertaken.

Environmental Groups' Training Needs in 30 Key Competencies

As defined by the American Society for Training and Development, training is "identifying, assessing and—through planned learning—helping develop key competencies which enable individuals to perform current or future jobs." Using this definition and recognizing the great diversity in environmental groups, The Conservation Foundation devised an assessment that measured the training needs in 30 key skills for all types of environmental staff—paid workers, both professional and clerical, full- or part-time, as well as members or volunteers. Divided into four broad categories, these skills include fund-raising and membership recruitment; internal management; communication and education; and policy development and research.

In the survey, training in all four categories was ranked as "high priority" or "somewhat needed" for staff by over 50 percent of the groups responding. The category of fund-raising and membership recruitment topped the list, with the three other broad categories clustered close together at a lower level of need.

Training needs in the internal management skills of "strategic planning" and "use of volunteers" were rated as a "high priority" by about one-third of all groups responding and as needed to some degree by nearly four-fifths of the groups. In the category of communication and education, a function common to all groups, roughly 25 percent of the groups rated as "high priority" the need for training in "press relations" and in the "editing and production of newsletters."

Of the groups surveyed, 38 percent are engaged in research; 45 percent are engaged in policy development. Thus, many of the groups considered training in substantive policy matters an important priority. Training in the "economics of environmental policies" was a need recognized by 63 percent of the respondents. New policy ideas were regarded as "badly needed" by 41 percent of the groups; another 41 percent thought they were "somewhat needed."

How Environmental Groups View the Importance of Training

Roughly one-sixth (16 percent) of the groups surveyed identified training as one of their most important needs; over 50 percent considered training important but not as important as other needs; over 25 percent thought the need for training was of relatively little importance.

About 50 percent of all the groups that responded to the questionnaire provide no training at all. (Of the groups with annual budgets under $1,000, 70 percent provide no training.) Moreover, training is often regarded as "gravy," the first item to be cut in a tight operating budget. Roughly a third of all the training budgets are under $500, although 18 percent are over $10,000. Groups with over 10,000 members are twice as likely as the average to provide some training for staff.

Only 5 percent of the groups responding to the survey said that the person who could benefit most from training would have no time for it. Among groups with memberships greater than 1,000 (that is, all but the smallest groups), 33 percent would send the appropriate staff member for a three- to six-day training course; 42 percent of groups with memberships between 10,000 and 100,000 would send a person for one or two weeks.

When queried about their knowledge of training resources, 50 percent of the groups did not know what resources were available to meet their needs. Information about practical, inexpensive programs was scarce. Presumably there is a need for tailored, in-house staff training programs as well as programs for executive leadership and management development. The training needs of grass-roots and volunteer groups, where leadership and responsibilities frequently change, obviously differ from those of the larger groups.

Training Resources

The research for this report identified a vast array of resources that deliver training. Often environmental groups themselves, in both ad hoc and annual meetings or at workshops, combine training with issue development.

There are many training books, manuals, and journals. Other potential training resources include traditional institutions such as the American Society for Training and Development (ASTD), the American Society for Association Executives (ASAE), and the American Management Association (AMA). Newer organizations, known as management support organizations (MSOs), nonprofits themselves, offer flexible training opportunities in a variety of cities for reasonable fees. A few opportunities provided by corporations and government are available. Also, community-organizing training centers are providers of training in advocacy skills. Indirectly, university graduate environmental studies programs may contribute to policy development training through symposia and institutes open to the larger community. Academic management training is available in master of business administration (MBA) or in public administration programs. On a number of campuses, growing interest in teaching nonprofit management in degree programs or in continuing education efforts is evident. Policy-oriented fellowships and internships are available through universities and foundations.

How to Improve Training in Environmental Groups—Recommendations

Based on the responses to the questionnaire, information obtained in interviews conducted for this report, and research into resources, several steps appear likely to improve the amount and quality of training that can be provided to environmental groups. The major recommendations of this report are as follows.

- Serious consideration should be given to establishing a national or regional clearinghouse to link the training needs of environmental groups to the resources available to meet these needs. A clearinghouse, guided by a steering committee of environmental organizations and training experts, could maintain a directory of resources, become an exchange or broker for materials and services, prepare bibliographies of training materials, and publish a newsletter.
- A meeting of environmental trainers to discuss the training needs identified by environmental groups would be useful.
- Private funding sources could provide money for a pilot program in policy training. This program, using a variety of techniques and media, could be developed and delivered by universities or environmental research organizations.
- There is a need for regular meetings among the deans of environmental studies programs. The deans could discuss common problems and concerns of their programs, the sharing of facilities such as field stations, and internships and job placement for students as well as career paths for graduates.
- Internships are an efficient training device and should be used more frequently. They can improve both the policy competence and the internal management of a group.
- Most of the existing management training resources have not been aimed at or used by environmental groups. Managers of medium-sized environmental groups can seek out various problem-solving programs for nonprofit managers. A two- or three-day training course on internal management subjects targeted to the larger environmental groups, and designed by several of them, might also be useful.

Conclusions

The great diversity of environmental groups, of training needs, and of methods and organizations to meet these needs makes it difficult to generalize about the appropriateness of training for environmental groups. However, it is clear from our research that the environmental community has needs for both management and policy training that are currently unmet.

The need for training is generally given lower priority by environmental groups than are other needs more obviously related to those organizations' programmatic goals. Environmental groups are often short of funds, and programmatic goals tend to take priority over more instrumental needs such as training. But training can improve the fund-raising skills of groups as well as increase the effectiveness and efficiency with which the funds are used.

Because most of the existing management training resources have not been aimed at or used by environmental groups, creating linkages is probably the most necessary step in management training. Improving both the policy skills and knowledge of environmental groups are also important: here, additional funding for policy training is probably the greatest need.

The steps that must be taken to meet training needs require money. Given the resource constraints of environmental groups and the priority that they give to programmatic goals, it is unlikely that environmental organizations will devote a significant part of their existing funds to training. Thus, if the management and policy skills of environmental groups are to be upgraded, new support from foundations, corporations, and the government will be necessary. We hope this report will stimulate, in both funding sources and environmental groups, more awareness of the training needs that exist.

Chapter 1

Introduction

Environmental groups have been long concerned with training. Yet most of their efforts, historically and recently, have been devoted to training others. Environmental groups may encourage programs in schools, at nature centers, or on television to develop greater awareness of ecological problems. This report does not focus on that kind of training, but rather on the training needs of members and staffs of environmental groups themselves.

The term *training* has many connotations. In this report, it is used largely as defined by the American Society for Training and Development: the focus of training and development is "identifying, assessing and—through planned learning—helping develop the key competencies which enable individuals to perform current or future jobs."[1]

There are several thousand environmental groups in the United States. They range from organizations with broad agendas addressed by a full-time staff of several hundred specialists to single-issue groups run by a few volunteers working in their spare time. The training needs of these groups vary widely.

Diversity of Environmental Groups

The environmental movement emerged during the 1960s as many different groups began to develop a sense of common goals. A few of these groups had been founded in the 19th century, but many were new. Their varied interests and concerns included recreation, conservation, natural history, pollution control, wildlife, forestry, health, and land use.[2]

Despite a sense of shared goals, environmental groups continue to reflect diversity. Even within the same group, there may be varying perspectives. As Byron Kennard, a long-time organizer in groups concerned with social change, including many environmental ones, has noted, such groups may be elitist or populist, national or grass roots, global or backyard, funded or unfunded; their staffs may be

1

composed of professionals or volunteers, experts or generalists, old-timers or young turks; and so on.[3]

Environmental groups in the United States have memberships ranging from zero to millions of people and budgets ranging from zero to millions of dollars. Perhaps half the groups are completely volunteer organizations; a few have several hundred paid staff members. Some groups are devoted to fish, birds, or tortoises; others lobby for worker health or population control. Some groups emphasize conservation and management of natural resources; others lean toward preservation. No specific issue is common to more than half of the groups; even if issues overlap, the means of addressing them may differ. Some groups litigate and work with the media; others publish technical journals and avoid advocacy. Groups working mainly at the opposite ends of the research-education-action spectrum are often uncomfortable being associated with one another.

In general, environmental groups can be placed in one of the following eight categories.

1. *Small, all-volunteer, education groups.* A group in this category has perhaps 300 to 600 members and a relatively low annual budget obtained from membership dues and sales of publications and other material. It is run entirely by a volunteer board, key members of which serve for many years. This type of group probably emphasizes interpretative activities focusing on a particular plant or animal and its habitat. Such groups are often long-established and may be regional or national in scope.

2. *Small, single-issue, activist groups.* This type of group is likely to have recruited several thousand members in its 10- to 20-year history. It addresses a single issue, for example, saving a particular piece or type of land—wilderness, wetlands, a neighborhood—through organizing, lobbying, and litigating. It may have several staffers, volunteer or paid. Its budget is in the $10,000 to $100,000 range, raised through direct mail campaigns as well as dues.

3. *Recreation and sport clubs.* These organizations generally have a long history. Members, perhaps several hundred, usually enjoy hunting or fishing. The focus is largely social, but such groups are active in protecting wildlife and habitat. Recreation and sport clubs tend to rely heavily on volunteers.

4. *Coordinating groups.* A coordinating group may operate at the state or regional level. Its membership numbers in the thousands, including many institutions as well as individuals. Several full-time staff are assisted by volunteers in performing such functions as lobbying in the state capital and educating people on key state land and

pollution issues. The budget probably runs between $100,000 and $200,000, mainly from dues and large donations.

5. *Education, communication, research, and policy development groups*. These groups focus on developing and communicating options for environmental policy. They may be either national or regional in scope. Established mainly in the past decade, these policy-oriented groups are often centers or institutes with constituencies but without dues-paying members, making fund-raising essential to support the research agenda. Budgets and size vary considerably.

6. *Litigating groups*. A litigating group is likely to work primarily at the national level, influencing legislative and administrative actions on pollution control and land use through a staff of professional lawyers, scientists, and economists. Several million dollars may be raised by such groups through direct mail campaigns and in foundation grants. Members usually play no active role in the program.

7. *National membership groups*. A national membership group typically has a long history in the conservation field and has millions of members in local groups. Much of its program provides services for these members, particularly educational materials and field experiences, although this kind of organization is also likely to be active in lobbying. The paid staff probably reaches several hundred, with volunteers into the thousands.

8. *Professional societies*. A professional society promotes research in the discipline it represents by holding conferences and publishing journals. Membership may run from 5,000 to 20,000. The society may or may not take policy stands. Its budget depends on the size of the group but comes from dues, publications, and conference fees and covers the salaries of its full-time employees.

The majority of environmental groups fit into one of these eight categories, but few fit perfectly and some not at all. There are groups with no members, groups that are coalitions of other organizations formed to handle a specific issue, and groups that function as clearinghouses, trainers, or expedition arrangers. The diversity of the environmental movement is one of its major strengths, but it also means that training needs and the ability to take advantage of training programs vary considerably, depending on a group's resources, concerns, and style.

Changing Conditions Mean New Training Needs

In the early years of the environmental movement, certain types of skills—working with the media, litigating landmark cases, lobbying for new laws—were especially valued. The 1980s have seen changes in political and economic conditions as well as in technology and environmental problems. The skills learned earlier remain important—sometimes, however, with new twists. For example, lobbying now usually involves overseeing and amending existing laws rather than writing legislation in entirely new areas. And one important way in which environmental groups can learn to deal with changing priorities in the movement is through training programs.

Changes in federal policy in the past few years have reduced federal funding of citizen environmental programs and influenced the type and availability of training needed by environmental groups. Fewer opportunities for government funding result in less need for training in how to write proposals for government grants. The demand is for training in other methods of raising funds.[4] There is a new or revived interest in creating business enterprises to support environmental groups.[5] Some groups are dealing with an increase in membership; others are facing a decline. Increased membership as a result of citizen concern has enlarged the need to train additional staff to handle the influx of members, particularly at the chapter level. In contrast, groups with stable or declining membership must upgrade skills of existing staff and are looking for more sophisticated training programs.

Some groups find that changing life-styles and social conditions make it much harder to find and retain volunteers. There is thus an increased need for recruitment and continued training in skills to handle the turnover. The League of Women Voters saw its membership—all active volunteers—drop by more than 25 percent during the 1970s, a trend now reversed partly by training in membership recruitment.[6]

The way in which issues are addressed by environmental groups and the way in which groups operate have also shifted. As a result of hard economic times and charges that environmental regulation is unproductive and costs jobs, a number of groups have begun to focus more sharply on the economic aspects of environmental questions. New training resources are being developed to help them.[7] Smaller groups are being forced to retrench, which means that courses in strategic planning, ignored in easier times, have gained importance. Shared space and mergers among groups are more common. Increased transportation costs make it more difficult to bring people together for training.

Political and economic conditions aside, environmental issues continue to change. For instance, air pollution concerns are moving from conventional pollutants to acid rain and indoor air contamination. Concern about hazardous waste has spawned new training and education programs. With pollution-control laws on the books, attention is turning toward improving how these laws work and finding ways to integrate environmental controls on substances that move from one part of the environment to another. The net result has been a need to strengthen the research and policy development capabilities of environmental groups.

Training in communication skills continues to be necessary, with new emphases emerging. In some situations, negotiation is being used to resolve both site-specific and policy disputes.[8] Members and staff of environmental groups are learning how to use negotiation effectively through training workshops and from participating in actual negotiations. Many groups, such as those interested in soil conservation and wildlife, need to improve their lobbying, networking, and press relations skills to ensure that their issues are addressed. Larger organizations are already using the records management and bibliographic research possibilities of the new computer technology. Mid-size groups are eager to do so. The computer's potential in networking and information exchange is beginning to be explored. Training in computer skills is becoming increasingly important.

The Conservation Foundation Report

To ascertain what training is needed by environmental groups, what training is being provided, what obstacles exist to obtaining training, and what initiatives, if any, are desirable, The Conservation Foundation studied the existing literature, solicited information by questionnaire, and interviewed leaders of environmental groups, providers of training, and sources of funding.

About 400 professional associations, communication, educational, and research organizations, and activist groups were selected to receive the questionnaire on training needs; 225 questionnaires were completed and returned. (The methodology and a description of the sample are included in appendix A.) To supplement the questionnaire responses, a number of interviews were conducted. Foundation President William K. Reilly talked with the heads of 14 major national environmental organizations. Project staff had numerous telephone and in-person discussions with other representatives and with providers of training for both environmental and nonenvironmental groups. Frequently, these interviews elicited a view of an organization different from the questionnaire response.

Not surprisingly, this research uncovered a variety of training needs and, surprisingly, a large number and variety of resources to meet those needs.

References

1. Patricia A. McLagan and David Bedrick, *Models for Excellence: The Results of the ASTD Training and Development Competency Study* (Washington, D.C.: ASTD, 1983).

2. The information in this and the following section was gleaned from responses to The Conservation Foundation questionnaire (see appendix B) as well as a review of the literature.

3. Byron Kennard, *Nothing Can Be Done, Everything Is Possible* (Andover, Mass.: Brick House Publishing, 1982), pp. 87-88.

4. See March/April 1983 issue of *Grantsmanship Center News*.

5. See Charles Cagnon, "Business Ventures of Citizen Groups," *The NRAG Papers*, (Helena, Mont.: Northern Rockies Action Group, 1982). (Available from Northern Rockies Action Group, 9 Placer, Helena, MT 59601.)

6. League of Women Voters, "Long-Range Planning," *Prospectus* 3:9.

7. See *Community Jobs* special issues, Vol. 3/No. 9, November 1980 and Vol.4/No. 9, November 1981. (Available from Community Jobs, 1520 Sixteenth St., N.W., Washington, DC 20036.)

8. See Allan R. Talbot, *Settling Things: Six Case Studies in Environmental Mediation* (Washington, D.C.: The Conservation Foundation and The Ford Foundation, 1983); *Resolve*, a newsletter on environmental dispute resolution (Available from The Conservation Foundation, 1717 Massachusetts Avenue, N.W., Washington, DC 20036.)

Chapter 2

Training Needs of Environmental Groups

This chapter, drawn largely from responses to The Conservation Foundation's questionnaire, describes the priority environmental groups give to the need for training in specific skills, the overall importance of training to these groups compared with their other needs, and the resources they are willing to use for training. A final section draws largely on the comments of leaders of national groups interviewed for this report.

Specific Training Needs

The Conservation Foundation questionnaire surveyed the importance of training in each of 30 skills "for which training could potentially be provided to a group like yours." The respondents were asked whether training in each skill for staff and members (as applicable)* was "a high-priority need," "somewhat needed," "not needed because skill is not important," or "not needed because training [is] already provided." (The questionnaire is appendix B of this report; the overall results, by percentage of groups marking each option for each skill, are presented in appendix C.)

There were only a handful of skills for which more than 25 percent of the groups indicated that training had already been provided. At 30 and 31 percent, respectively, "accounting" and "library

---

* Only about half as many respondents rated member needs as rated staff needs. There may be several reasons for this. About 20 percent of the groups have no members; many others have members only in the sense of financial contributors. There was also some confusion among respondents whether to equate members and volunteers, although volunteers are often part of the staff. Because of the relatively few responses and the confusion over definition, this chapter primarily discusses staff needs. Member needs are included in appendix C, however. As table 2.1 indicates, high-priority needs for members were generally slightly lower in all categories except fund-raising and membership recruitment, where they were considerably lower.

services and information retrieval" were the highest. Some skills were regarded as "not important" by a large proportion of the groups. For example, 68 percent rated "participation in electoral campaigns" as not important; over 50 percent put "litigaton" in this category (see table 2.16). Management skills as a whole were less likely to be considered important by the smallest groups, which usually have no staff and low budgets.

The 30 skills covered can be divided into four general types: fund-raising and membership recruitment, internal management, communication and education, and policy development and research.* Table 2.1 shows how the respondents ranked training needs in these four areas. In all four categories of skills, the need for training was ranked as "high priority" or "somewhat needed" for staff by over half the groups responding. Fund-raising and membership recruitment skills topped the list, with the other three categories of skills grouped together at a lower level of need. Priorities for training varied considerably from skill to skill within each of the four categories.

Fund-raising and Membership Recruitment

Table 2.2 shows ratings of two training needs related to membership recruitment and three related to fund-raising: "direct mail to recruit new members" and "other techniques for membership recruiting"; "fund-raising through direct mail," "obtaining government and foundation grants," and "other methods for raising funds." "Other techniques for membership recruiting" and "other methods for raising funds" ranked highest among the training needs of the groups surveyed. Around 80 percent said their staff needs this type of training. (In fact, among the 30 skills covered, only training in the "use of volunteers, interns" and for "long-range planning, strategic planning" received percentages this high.) The "high-priority" figures for the other three items in this group are probably deflated because over 10 percent of the groups now provide training.

The need for training in "other techniques for membership recruiting" seems to be most keenly felt by the smallest groups (table 2.3). Training in this area is aready provided by 33 percent of the

---

* Scientific training in many disciplines is often needed by environmental groups. The Conservation Foundation did not survey this type of training, which is provided by universities, professional associations, and journals. Efforts have been made by the National Science Foundation, for example, to link citizens and scientific information. Scientists also play an important role in some environmental groups as members.

Table 2.1

**Importance of Four Types of Training Needs
by Average Percentage of Groups**

Skill	For Staff		For Members	
	High Priority	Combined High Priority; Somewhat Needed	High Priority	Combined High Priority; Somewhat Needed
Fund-raising and membership recruitment	39	71	24	50
Internal management	18	57	12	35
Policy development and research	17	53	15	48
Communication and education	16	51	14	45

Table 2.2

**Fund-raising and Membership Recruitment Training Needs for Staff
by Overall Percentage of Groups**

Skill	High Priority	Somewhat Needed	Combined High Priority and Somewhat Needed	Skill Not Important	Training Provided
Other techniques for membership recruiting	49	30	(79)	14	8
Other methods for raising funds	46	34	(80)	10	9
Direct mail to recruit new members	37	30	(67)	17	16
Fund-raising through direct mail	33	29	(62)	19	19
Obtaining government and foundation grants	32	35	(67)	19	13

Table 2.3

**Fund-raising and Membership Recruitment Training Needs for Staff
by Size of Group Membership (percentage)**

	1-1,000	1,001-10,000	10,001-100,000	More than 100,001
Fund-raising through direct mail	33/26*	38/36	33/22	33/0
Obtaining government and foundation grants	40/25	29/46	17/44	22/22
Other methods for raising funds	43/34	45/38	61/28	56/11
Direct mail to recruit new members	48/31	35/38	47/18	22/11
Other techniques for membership recruiting	64/24	44/44	56/28	33/33

*Thirty-three percent of groups rated skills as "a high-priority need"; 26 percent rated skill as "somewhat needed."

largest membership groups; another 33 percent rate it a "high-priority" need. Some professional societies may find their membership static or decreasing; a state group may want to strengthen its work by organizing local chapters; a natural history group may need revitalization. The greater need of smaller membership groups presumably results from the major success of larger activist groups in the past few years. The Sierra Club has doubled its membership, growing more in 1981-82 than it did after Earth Day. However, other groups have not fared as well in tough competition for members and funding.[1]

The largest high-priority need for training in "other methods for raising funds" is among mid-size groups—those with memberships between 10,001 and 100,000 and budgets between $50,001 and $100,000 (tables 2.3 and 2.4). The overall need for training in obtaining grants is greatest for somewhat smaller groups; 40 percent of the smallest membership groups ranked this as a high priority. The high-priority need for training in direct mail fund-raising is more evenly distributed among groups of different sizes.

Table 2.4

Fund-raising and Membership Recruitment Training Needs for Staff by Budget Size (Percentage)

	$100-$1,000	$1,001-$10,000	$10,001-$50,000	$50,001-$100,000	$100,001-$600,000	More than $600,001
Fund-raising through direct mail	31/19*	33/26	35/38	33/20	33/40	32/18
Obtaining government and foundation grants	15/15	24/27	38/46	29/50	34/39	29/34
Other methods for raising funds	14/21	39/27	52/36	63/25	45/50	47/29
Direct mail to recruit new members	43/36	43/36	40/32	27/13	34/34	37/29
Other techniques for membership recruiting	57/29	56/26	57/26	57/14	40/38	44/38

*Thirty-one percent of groups rate need as high priority/19 percent rate need as somewhat needed.

The 5 skills in the fund-raising and membership recruitment category are the top 5 among the 30 rated in an overall ranking of "high-priority" training needs ("fund-raising through direct mail," at 42 percent, tied with "use of volunteers, interns") (see table 2.14). They rank nearly as high when "high priority" and "somewhat needed" are combined (see table 2.18).

Internal Management

Environmental groups are almost always started and run by people concerned about the issues. These individuals may well bring scientific, advocacy, and other skills as well as knowledge of the issue to an organization, but it has been a matter of luck whether they also have brought skill and interest in management. The need for administrative skills often does not go unrecognized. Rather, staff and members may not be as interested in acquiring these skills as others and may feel there are insufficient funds to hire people who already possess them.

A report on volunteers in environmental groups prepared in 1972 notes that leaders and volunteers are intensely focused on goals; they move from crisis to crisis, leaving neither the time nor energy, or sometimes the inclination, to tend to the tasks that can assure long-term viability and increased influence for their organizations.[2] Authored 10 years later, the report of a national meeting of community land trusts states that participants were often more comfortable talking about land-saving techniques, such as easements and tax regulations, than about such institutional skills as administration or building community support. One long-time environmental leader commented in an interview with The Conservation Foundation that in both large organizations in which he has worked "street fighters are now doing management, and they don't know how." Another observed, "Environmental activists rather than management people are in power, and they don't even know what they're missing."

Table 2.5 shows the results from The Conservation Foundation's survey on questions dealing with management training needs. In an overall ranking of "high-priority" training needs in the 30 skills, the management skills fall as follows: (4) "use of volunteers, interns"; (6) "long-range planning, strategic planning"; (8) "use of office technology (i.e., word-processing, etc.)"; (19) "budgeting"; (21) "accounting and financial management"; and (22) "board-staff relations," "office management, including supervisory skills," and "per-

Table 2.5

Management Training Needs for Staff by Percentage of Groups

Skill	High Priority	Somewhat Needed	Combined High Priority and Somewhat Needed	Skill Not Important	Training Provided
Use of volunteers, interns	33	45	(78)	10	12
Long-range planning, strategic planning	32	47	(79)	12	10
Use of office technology (i.e., word processing, etc.)	25	33	(58)	26	16
Budgeting	14	43	(57)	16	27
Accounting and financial management	13	43	(56)	15	30
Board-staff relations	12	38	(50)	32	18
Office management, including supervisory skills	12	40	(52)	29	19
Personnel management, including hiring, staffing patterns, and staff benefits	12	32	(44)	35	22

sonnel management, including hiring, staffing patterns, and staff benefits" (see table 2.14).

If training is or already has been provided, then the assumption might be made that an organization regards such training as a high priority. Even so, if the "high-priority" and "already provided" responses are combined, the rankings of the management skills, in the order given above and in table 2.5, are (7), (14), (15), (15), (10), (27), (26), and (20), respectively (see table 2.19). That is, mostly, they are on the bottom half of the list. Note that, in this ranking, "accounting and financial management," at (10), falls at the same level as "press relations" and "library services and information retrieval." And these three rank below all of the fund-raising and membership recruitment skills as well as such skills as "editing and production of newsletters" and "relating to state and local government."

When the responses indicating that training is a "high priority" or is "somewhat needed" are combined, two skills in the management category—"use of volunteers, interns" and "long-range planning, strategic planning"—rise to the top of the list of 30 skills, at (4) and (2), respectively (see table 2.18). These are a high priority for a third of all groups; nearly four-fifths of all groups indicated some need for them. Regardless of individual characteristics, environmental groups apparently perceive training in these two skills as a way to cope with the funding crunch.

Strategic planning skills are in place for only 10 percent of the groups and skills in working with volunteers for 12 percent of the groups (table 2.5). About 90 percent of the groups with budgets between $50,001 and $600,000 said training in strategic planning is needed. It is a high priority for 60 percent of groups with budgets between $50,001 and $100,000 and memberships between 10,001 and 100,000 (tables 2.6 and 2.7). Generally, the need is large for these two skills regardless of a group's issue, function, size, or location, although for the smaller membership groups the need is secondary rather than a high priority.

Training in working with volunteers is needed not only because of the harder economic times; it is also a means of bridging the gap between paid staff and grass-roots volunteers. The leader of a national group in an interview for this report noted:

Training in humanism is needed in membership organizations so that volunteers are better valued. The attitude among professionals is that volunteers are cannon fodder to be pushed for letters and telegrams. They should be encouraged and thanked for writing letters. The arrogance of lob-

Table 2.6

**Management Training Needs for Staff
by Size of Membership (Percentage)**

	1-1,000	1,001-10,000	10,001-100,000	More than 100,000
Accounting and financial management	15/40*	8/48	24/47	22/24
Board-staff relations	5/33	12/44	22/50	33/22
Budgeting	12/39	12/42	17/72	25/38
Office management, including supervisory skills	3/26	16/47	25/69	25/38
Personnel management, including hiring, staffing patterns, and staff benefits	5/16	12/40	22/67	22/33
Long-range planning, strategic planning	32/42	23/60	61/28	33/33
Use of office technology (i.e., word-processing, etc.)	20/17	29/45	37/53	25/25
Use of volunteers, interns	41/30	26/56	32/58	33/44

*Fifteen percent of the groups rated skill as a "high-priority need"; 40 percent rated skill as "somewhat needed."

byists relating to constituencies is a particular problem of the big membership groups. We badly need a formal training process to relate these two groups to each other.

Budgeting, accounting, office management, and board-staff relations were more likely to be rated "somewhat needed" rather than "a high-priority need," but over 50 percent of the groups that responded to the questionnaire said they could benefit from at least some training in these areas. Training in board-staff relations increases as a priority by membership group size. About a third of the groups headquartered in Washington, D.C., see it as a high-priority need

Table 2.7

Management Training Needs for Staff by Budget Size (Percentage)

	$100- $1,000	$1,001- $10,000	$10,001- $50,000	$50,001- $100,000	$100,001- $600,000	More than $600,000
Accounting and financial management	7/29*	13/31	4/57	21/29	12/55	16/43
Board-staff relations	0/23	3/26	10/43	7/47	15/49	21/42
Budgeting	7/21	13/28	10/55	7/47	20/46	16/51
Office management, including supervisory skills	0/15	3/8	13/35	29/29	7/62	21/62
Personnel management, including hiring, staffing patterns, and staff benefits	0/0	5/3	0/23	29/36	10/52	21/47
Long-range planning, strategic planning	17/58	21/42	38/42	62/31	27/66	44/38
Use of office technology (i.e., word processing, etc.)	7/7	11/8	28/32	38/31	24/45	37/47
Use of volunteers, interns	29/43	45/25	36/45	44/38	14/69	38/41

*Seven percent of the groups rated skill as "a high-priority need"; 29 percent rated skill as "somewhat needed."

for both members and staff. The need for training in the use of office technology is found primarily among larger membership groups; 50 percent of the groups with over 100,000 members already have this type of training and the other 50 percent expressed a need for it.

Around 90 percent or more of the groups with 10,001 to 100,000 members expressed a need for training in office technology, office management, budgeting, and personnel management. Several factors may result in especially high needs for these organizations. Some may have been created largely by a few individuals in the early 1970s and now need to change their leadership structure and acquire additional skills to cope with changing times. Existing skills in issues and communications may no longer be enough if the groups have grown significantly. These groups also probably have fewer resources to meet their needs.

Management problems are not limited to newer groups, of course. An older group responding to the questionnaire noted it was more oriented toward putting out brushfires than setting achievable goals and working to meet them. The lack of strategy skills makes it difficult for this or any group to budget and make personnel decisions. And a manager of a major national group said in an interview:

> Time management, familiarity with office equipment, comfortable use of computers, and the management of people are all serious deficiencies in this organization and in many nonprofits. We could all use instruction in supervisory skills. Board-staff relations are a critical need that no one addresses head-on. Problems and poor communication are allowed to fester. Training could provide a way to address these concerns, to get issues out on the table, in the open, without a crisis having to provoke it.

Communications and Education

Education and communication are functions common to all of the groups replying to The Conservation Foundation's questionnaire. Some skills in this area are valued by almost all groups (table 2.8). "Press relations" and "editing and production of newsletters," for example, are skills deemed unimportant by only about 10 percent of the groups surveyed. About 25 percent of the groups said they have "high-priority" training needs in these two areas as well as in the less frequently needed skills of "editing, production, and marketing of books and pamphlets."

At the other end of the spectrum are "participation in electoral campaigns" and "litigation," the skills ranked (1) and (2) in unimportance among the 30 skills surveyed (see table 2.16). Litigation train-

Table 2.8

Communication Training Needs for Staff by Percentage of Groups

Skill	High Priority	Somewhat Needed	Combined High Priority and Somewhat Needed	Skill Not Important	Training Provided
Editing and production of newsletters	25	38	(63)	9	28
Press relations	24	46	(70)	11	19
Editing, production, and marketing of books and pamphlets	23	32	(55)	27	18
Relating to state or local government	23	36	(59)	10	23
Local group organizing	19	36	(55)	30	15
Networking with other groups, coalition building	15	44	(59)	19	22
Lobbying	14	34	(48)	29	24
Conference planning and management	12	47	(59)	21	20
Relating to federal government	11	40	(51)	28	21
Use of mediation and negotiation for environmental disputes	9	36	(45)	46	9
Participation in electoral campaigns	7	17	(24)	68	9
Litigation	6	21	(27)	55	18

ing was not considered important for staff in 55 percent of the groups; moreover, of the remaining 45 percent, 18 percent already had staff trained in litigation. The overall reported need for training in litigating skills is a good bit higher in the South (48 percent) and West (37 percent), perhaps because most of the main litigating groups are now located in the East. No responding groups in the South, for example, had staff trained in litigation.

Two-thirds of the respondents indicated that "participation in electoral campaigns" is not an important skill for either members or staff. However, the need for training in this area did interest activist groups in some regions of the country. Among groups in the West, it is "a high-priority need" for members in more than 25 percent of the groups. This may be the result of the Sierra Club's focus on electoral participation.

More "high-priority" interest in training in the "use of mediation and negotiation for environmental disputes" is also found in the West. Among western groups, 32 percent listed dispute resolution techniques as a high priority for members and 20 percent noted it for staff. This may be because western groups have longer experience with mediation than groups in other parts of the country: several leading environmental mediation groups have been active in the West, including the Mediation Institute in Seattle, Washington, and AC-CORD Associates in Boulder, Colorado. Nearly half of all groups, however, said that skills in this are not needed.

"Relating to state and local government" is one of the few areas in which the need expressed for training members slightly exceeded the need for training staff. Along with "local group organizing," it ranked first in training needs in communication skills for members (considering only "high-priority" ratings). The two were rated high priority by 25 percent of the groups. Among groups with 10,001 to 100,000 members, 50 percent rated training for members in relating to state and local government a high priority. The relatively high priority attached to training for the state or local, rather than federal, level may reflect a belief that action on environmental issues is now taking place there as well as the fact that many groups are state and local in focus.

In comments on the questionnaire, "networking with other groups, coalition building" was often suggested as a crucial need to increase the effectiveness of environmental groups and avoid duplication of effort. Networking and "conference planning and management," one way of providing the opportunity to network, ranked third, along with "relating to state or local governments," among communications skills for which staff were thought to need training.

Tables 2.9 and 2.10 show these needs for staff by membership and budget size. Among the top-ranked skills, training needs seem to be greatest in the smallest membership groups (1 to 1,000 members) and in those with 10,001 to 100,000 members. As noted previously, the latter groups often expressed the greatest desire for training. It should be noted, too, that in the largest membership groups training fre-

---

Table 2.9

**Communication Training Needs for Staff
by Size of Membership (Percentage)**

	1-1,000	1,001-10,000	10,001-100,000	More than 100,000
Editing and production of newsletters	34/31*	15/51	25/38	0/33
Press relations	29/43	21/45	39/44	13/25
Editing, production, and marketing of books and pamphlets	27/22	21/44	29/35	11/44
Relating to state or local government	31/35	13/38	29/18	25/0
Local group organizing	16/30	8/52	41/18	22/22
Networking with other groups, coalition building	18/43	13/44	12/41	0/33
Lobbying	21/25	9/43	6/29	11/33
Conference planning and management	13/44	8/51	18/41	0/33
Relating to the federal government	17/40	4/43	18/35	11/22
Use of mediation and negotiation for environmental disputes	16/31	4/44	6/35	0/33
Participation in electoral campaigns	11/18	2/18	7/0	25/0
Litigation	8/21	0/24	12/24	11/0

*Thirty-four percent of the groups rated skill as "a high-priority need"; 31 percent rated skill as "somewhat needed."

Table 2.10

Communication Training Needs for Staff by Size of Budget (Percentage)

	$100-$1,000	$1,001-$10,000	$10,001-$50,000	$50,001-$100,000	$100,001-$600,000	Over $600,000
Editing and production of newsletters	14/50*	33/38	32/36	25/50	14/40	16/39
Press relations	17/50	28/46	23/50	13/47	23/48	26/42
Editing, production, and marketing of books and pamphlets	8/23	27/22	13/43	29/14	19/40	24/42
Relating to state or local government	33/25	33/33	27/58	8/31	22/32	16/32
Local group organizing	23/38	23/36	22/30	0/55	18/35	18/37
Networking with other groups, coalition building	8/46	20/44	21/46	13/47	12/46	11/42
Lobbying	8/46	23/28	16/32	0/43	7/39	13/34
Conference planning and management	8/50	15/50	14/59	20/40	5/52	11/42
Relating to the federal government	25/33	18/37	4/54	14/29	7/40	13/41
Use of mediation and negotiation for environmental disputes	8/42	18/26	9/43	8/31	5/43	3/32
Participation in electoral campaigns	0/17	8/24	0/23	13/7	0/22	11/6
Litigation	7/21	5/25	0/27	7/20	3/23	11/13

*Fourteen percent of the groups rated skill as "a high-priority need"; 50 percent rated skill as "somewhat needed."

quently is not needed because it has already been provided: for example, in 75 percent of these groups for "relating to state or local government," in 67 percent for "relating to the federal government" and for "editing and production of newsletters," in 63 percent for "press relations," and in 56 percent for "lobbying" and "litigation." As to budget size, the greatest training needs in the top-ranked skills seem to be felt among groups with budgets ranging from $1,001 to $50,000, although groups with budgets over $100,000 also showed a strong interest in "press relations" and those over $600,000 in "editing, production, and marketing of books and pamphlets" (which is not a high priority in the groups with $10,001 to $50,000 budgets).

Communications skills continue to be very important for environmental groups. However, if one adds the "high-priority" and "training already provided" responses, under the assumption that the latter may indicate the fulfillment of a "high-priority need," only 4 out of 13, or 33 percent, of the communication skills fall in the top half of the list of 30 skills—compared with 5 out of 5, or 100 percent, in the fund-raising and membership recruitment category; 5 out of 8, or 62.5 percent, in the management category; and 3 out of 5, or 60 percent, in the research and policy category (see table 2.18).

Research and Policy Development

The many types of activities that may be considered research make it difficult to interpret training needs in this area. "How to research an issue" might mean how to take a community survey of where political power lies or how to prepare a study of local uses of hazardous substances and the appropriate disposal methods for hazardous wastes. Some people may mean employing the techniques of an investigative reporter. Others may assume that research training means learning to use the methods of any one of the increasingly numerous disciplines that relate to environmental policy. Among the many that may be relevant are engineering, economics, biology, ecology, epidemiology, and law. In fact, researching an issue may require an understanding of all these forms of research.

Policy briefings are probably the major way in which the information necessary to develop policy options is transferred. These briefings now occur at many meetings of professional associations, conferences run by some commercial firms specializing in publication of government policy information, and occasionally at universities. Although such briefings serve the needs of some policy researchers, the smaller activist groups often do not have access to them; it is these groups that have been hit most severely by cutbacks in government-funded citizen participation programs, which were important channels for the exchange of both policy and technical information.

Among the skills in the research and policy development category, training in the "economics of environmental policies" had the highest combined rating for "high priority" and "somewhat needed" (table 2.11). This high rating probably results from a desire to understand the arguments of proponents of government regulation, on one hand, and of market-type incentives, on the other, as well as from a desire by groups to do their own analysis of the environmental-economic nexus. Although more than 25 percent of the groups said that background policy briefings are not important for them, 15 percent gave them high priority.

Most of the items in this category come through as strong secondary needs. Tables 2.12 and 2.13 show responses by membership and budget size. The greatest interest in policy training was expressed by groups with large numbers of active members.

The need for good information access by some groups was also expressed in individual comments. A staff member of a Midwest health group stressed the difficulty of getting good toxic substance information. The director of a state group who spent a sabbatical at Yale as a Mellon Fellow commented how his experience underscored "how little we really know about the issues we are supposed to know well. . . . At the very least we need to find a way to subscribe to several dozen journals I now know about even though some of them cost from $200 to $500 a year."

Concern about policy was also reflected in the responses to another question in The Conservation Foundation survey: "Do you think that new policy ideas need to be developed to address the environmental problems faced by the U.S. and the world or do you think we already know what needs to be done?" Among those responding to this question, 41 percent thought that new policy ideas were "badly needed" and another 41 percent that they were "somewhat needed."

Six Rankings of the 30 Surveyed Skills

Tables 2.14 through 2.17 show how the 30 skills in question rank under each option in the questionnaire. The skills at the top of the list in table 2.16 were considered the *least important* by groups that responded; presumably, the skills at the bottom of the list are most important. Table 2.18 combines the "high-priority need" and

Table 2.11

Research and Policy Training Needs for Staff by Percentage of Groups

	High Priority	Somewhat Needed	Combined High Priority and Somewhat Needed	Skill Not Important	Training Provided
Particular policy issues (please specify)	22	20	(42)	39	21
Economics of environmental policies	21	42	(63)	24	13
How to research an issue	16	41	(57)	16	28
Background briefings on policy issues	15	41	(56)	27	18
Library services and information retrieval	12	35	(47)	23	31

Table 2.12

**Research and Policy Training Needs for Staff
by Size of Membership (Percentage)**

	1-1,000	1,001-10,000	10,001-100,000	More than 100,000
Particular policy issues (please specify)	22/19*	4/29	44/33	33/0
Economics of environmental policies	27/42	13/52	29/41	33/11
How to research an issue	21/33	12/50	20/40	11/22
Background briefings on policy issues	19/41	10/54	18/24	11/11
Library services and information retrieval	11/34	12/35	25/25	11/22

*Twenty-two percent of the groups rated skill as "a high-priority need"; 19 percent
rated skill as "somewhat needed."

"somewhat needed" responses. Table 2.19 combines the "high-priority" and "training already provided" responses.

Beyond what has been said about these rankings in the preceding pages, it is noteworthy that 8 of the top 10 "high-priority" training needs (table 2.14) are among the lowest skills in the "training already provided" category (table 2.17), ranking from 20 to 30. Also, although environmental groups are often associated with "participation in electoral campaigns" and "litigation," these skills topped the unimportant list for responding groups as a whole (table 2.16).

Overall Priority of Training

The priority that the groups surveyed placed on training compared with other needs is reflected both in their responses to a question on the overall importance of training and by the extent to which they now perform training or allocate their resources for this purpose.

Overall Importance of Training

In response to the question on overall importance, 16 percent of the groups indicated that they consider training to be one of their most

Table 2.13

**Research and Policy Needs for Staff
by Size of Budget (Percentage)**

	$100-$1,000	$1,001-$10,000	$10,001-$50,000	$50,001-$100,000	$100,001-$600,000	Over $600,000
Particular policy issues (please specify)	14/29*	14/14	30/20	9/45	17/29	25/10
Economics of environmental policies	14/71	20/48	32/40	14/43	13/58	24/30
How to research an issue	21/43	24/37	22/30	8/54	5/51	14/41
Background briefings on policy issues	21/50	18/38	18/45	27/33	5/63	16/22
Library services and information retrieval	8/23	13/28	13/54	0/31	10/24	17/39

*Fourteen percent of the groups rated skill as "a high-priority need"; 29 percent rated skill as "somewhat needed."

Table 2.14

Training Is a "High-Priority Need"

Skill	Percent Responding	Rank
Other techniques for membership recruiting	49	1
Other methods for raising funds	46	2
Direct mail to recruit new members	37	3
Fund-raising through direct mail	33	4
Use of volunteers, interns	33	4
Obtaining government and foundation grants	32	6
Long-range planning, strategic planning	32	6
Editing and production of newsletters	25	8
Use of office technology (i.e., word-processing, etc.)	25	8
Press relations	24	10
Editing, production, and marketing of books and pamphlets	23	11
Relating to state or local government	23	11
Particular policy issues (please specify)	22	13
Economics of environmental policies	21	14
Local group organizing	19	15
How to research an issue	16	16
Background briefings on policy issues	15	17
Networking with other groups, coalition building	15	17
Lobbying	14	19
Budgeting	14	19
Accounting and financial management	13	21
Board-staff relations	12	22
Office management, including supervisory skills	12	22
Personnel management, including hiring, staffing patterns, and staff benefits	12	22
Library services and information retrieval	12	22
Conference planning and management	12	22
Relating to the federal government	11	27
Use of mediation and negotiation for environmental disputes	9	28
Participation in electoral campaigns	7	29
Litigation	6	30

Table 2.15

Training Is "Somewhat Needed"

Skill	Percent Responding	Rank
Conference planning and management	47	1
Long-range planning, strategic planning	47	1
Press relations	46	3
Use of volunteers, interns	45	4
Networking with other groups, coalition building	44	5
Budgeting	43	6
Accounting and financial management	43	6
Economics of environmental policies	42	8
How to research an issue	41	9
Background briefings on policy issues	41	9
Relating to the federal government	40	11
Office management, including supervisory skills	40	11
Board-staff relations	38	13
Editing and production of newsletters	38	13
Relating to state or local government	36	15
Local group organizing	36	15
Use of mediation and negotiation for environmental disputes	36	15
Library services and information retrieval	35	18
Obtaining government and foundation grants	35	18
Other methods for raising funds	34	20
Lobbying	34	20
Use of office technology (i.e., word-processing, etc.)	33	22
Personnel management, including hiring, staffing patterns, and staff benefits	32	23
Editing, production, and marketing of books and pamphlets	32	23
Other techniques for membership recruiting	30	25
Direct mail to recruit new members	30	26
Fund-raising through direct mail	29	27
Litigation	21	28
Particular policy issues (please specify)	20	29
Participation in electoral campaigns	17	30

Table 2.16

Training Not Needed Because "Skill Not Important"

Skill	Percent Responding	Rank
Participation in electoral campaigns	68	1
Litigation	55	2
Use of mediation and negotiation for environmental disputes	46	3
Particular policy issues (please specify)	39	4
Personnel management, including hiring, staffing patterns, and staff benefits	35	5
Board-staff relations	32	6
Local group organizing	30	7
Lobbying	29	8
Office management, including supervisory skills	29	8
Relating to the federal government	28	10
Editing, production, and marketing of books and pamphlets	27	11
Background briefings on policy issues	27	11
Use of office technology (i.e., word-processing, etc.)	26	13
Economics of environmental policies	24	14
Library services and information retrieval	23	15
Conference planning and management	21	16
Networking with other groups, coalition building	19	17
Fund-raising through direct mail	19	17
Obtaining government and foundation grants	19	17
Direct mail to recruit new members	17	20
Budgeting	16	21
How to research an issue	16	21
Accounting and financial management	15	23
Other techniques for membership recruiting	14	24
Long-range planning, strategic planning	12	25
Press relations	11	26
Relating to state or local government	10	27
Use of volunteers, interns	10	27
Other methods for raising funds	10	27
Editing and production of newsletters	9	30

Table 2.17

Training Not Needed Because "Already Provided"

Skill	Percent Responding	Rank
Library services and information retrieval	31	1
Accounting and financial management	30	2
How to research an issue	28	3
Editing and production of newsletters	28	3
Budgeting	27	5
Lobbying	24	6
Relating to state or local government	23	7
Personnel management, including hiring, staffing patterns, and staff benefits	22	8
Networking with other groups, coalition building	22	8
Particular policy issues (please specify)	21	10
Relating to the federal government	21	10
Conference planning and management	20	12
Office management, including supervisory skills	19	13
Press relations	19	13
Fund-raising through direct mail	19	13
Litigation	18	16
Editing, production, and marketing of books and pamphlets	18	16
Board-staff relations	18	16
Background briefings on policy issues	18	16
Use of office technology (i.e., word-processing, etc.)	16	20
Direct mail to recruit new members	16	20
Local group organizing	15	22
Economics of environmental policies	13	23
Obtaining government and foundation grants	13	23
Use of volunteers, interns	12	25
Long-range planning, strategic planning	10	26
Other methods for raising funds	9	27
Use of mediation and negotiation for environmental disputes	9	27
Participation in electoral campaigns	9	27
Other techniques for membership recruiting	8	30

Table 2.18

Combined "High-Priority" and "Somewhat Needed"

Skill	Percent Responding	Rank
Other methods for raising funds	80	1
Other techniques for membership recruiting	79	2
Long-range planning, strategic planning	79	2
Use of volunteers, interns	78	4
Press relations	70	5
Direct mail to recruit new members	67	6
Obtaining government and foundation grants	67	6
Economics of environmental policies	63	8
Editing and production of newsletters	63	8
Fund-raising through direct mail	62	10
Relating to state or local government	59	11
Networking with other groups, coalition building	59	11
Conference planning and management	59	11
Use of office technology (i.e., word-processing, etc.)	58	14
Budgeting	57	15
How to research an issue	57	15
Background briefings on policy issues	56	17
Accounting and financial management	56	17
Editing, production, and marketing of books and pamphlets	55	19
Local group organizing	55	19
Office management, including supervisory skills	52	21
Relating to the federal government	51	22
Board-staff relations	50	23
Lobbying	48	24
Library services and information retrieval	47	25
Use of mediation and negotiation for environmental disputes	45	26
Personnel management, including hiring, staffing patterns, and staff benefits	44	27
Particular policy issues (please specify)	42	28
Litigation	27	29
Participation in electoral campaigns	24	30

Table 2.19

Combined "High-Priority" and "Training Provided"

Skill	Combined Percent	Rank
Other techniques for membership recruiting	57	1
Other methods for raising funds	55	2
Direct mail to recruit new members	53	3
Editing and production of newsletters	53	3
Fund-raising through direct mail	52	5
Relating to state or local government	46	5
Obtaining government and foundation grants	45	7
Use of volunteers, interns	45	7
How to research an issue	44	9
Library services and information retrieval	43	10
Particular policy issues (please specify)	43	10
Accounting and financial management	43	10
Press relations	43	10
Long-range planning, strategic planning	42	14
Use of office technology (i.e., word-processing, etc.)	41	15
Budgeting	41	15
Editing, production, and marketing of books and pamphlets	41	15
Lobbying	38	18
Networking with other groups, coalition building	37	19
Economics of environmental policies	34	20
Personnel management, including hiring, staffing patterns, and staff benefits	34	20
Local group organizing	34	22
Background briefings on policy issues	33	23
Conference planning and management	32	24
Relating to the federal government	32	24
Office management, including supervisory skills	31	26
Board-staff relations	30	27
Litigation	24	28
Use of mediation and negotiation for environmental disputes	18	29
Participation in electoral campaigns	16	30

important needs; 56 percent thought it an important need, but not as important as some others; 28 percent considered it not very important or of little importance (table 2.20).

A review of the top two "high-priority" training needs in each of the four categories of skills discussed above reveals that training is more likely to be a "high priority" for groups with no full-time staff. The "somewhat needed" figures are usually higher for groups that do have full-time staff. This is supported by the ratings of these groups on the importance of training in general (table 2.20). The major difference is that twice as many groups without full-time staff rated training as one of their most important needs. Groups with staff are more likely to see training as a secondary need, perhaps because some groups have staffers who are already trained and have the resources to get more training. Among groups with full-time staff, 35 percent said they have training budgets; only 10 percent of groups with no full-time staff do. Also, 58 percent of groups with full-time staff know who can meet their training needs, while only 36 percent of those without full-time staff do.

Table 2.20 also shows how group size relates to the importance placed on training. Over 75 percent of the groups with 10,001 to 100,000 members rated training as important, but not as important as some other needs. Training rated as a most important need for about a fifth of the groups regardless of budget category, except for groups with budgets between $100,001 and $600,000, where only 7 percent gave it a high priority.

Training Being Provided

About half of all the groups surveyed provide no training of any kind. The percentage reached 70 percent for groups with annual budgets under $1,000. However, about a fourth of the respondents said they provide some type of meetings or workshops for their members or the public, and about 30 percent provide some kind of training for their staff. Groups with over 10,000 members were twice as likely as the average to provide some training for staff (60 percent). Presumably some smaller groups are used to operating with skills acquired in other groups or careers and do not see training as needed or as a possibility given their resources.

Three-fourths of the groups had no funds in their budget for training. The percentage of groups with training budgets and the size of training budgets both increase as the membership of a group increases. Only 13 percent of the smallest organizations reported having such

Table 2.20

Overall Importance of Training Needs (Percentage)

One of our most important needs	16
Important, but not as important as some of our other needs	56
Not very important	21
Of little importance	7

Staff

	Full-time Staff	No Full-time Staff
One of our most important needs	11	23
Important, but not as important as some of our other needs	59	51
Not very important	22	19
Of little importance	8	7

Budget

	$100-$1,000	$1,001-$10,000	$10,001-$50,000	$50,001-$100,000	$100,001-$600,000	Over $600,000
One of our most important needs	21	20	20	18	7	18
Important, but not as important as some of our others	50	47	60	59	61	66
Not very important	21	24	17	24	27	8
Of little importance	7	8	3	—	5	8

Membership (Percentage)

	1-1,000	1,001-10,000	10,001-100,000	Over 100,000
One of our most important needs	14	22	17	22
Important, but not as important as some of our others	58	48	78	67
Not very important	19	26	6	11
Of little importance	9	3	—	—

budgets; over 70 percent of the largest groups did. On a functional basis, groups for which community organizing is important had the highest percentage of training budgets (42 percent), reflecting the importance training has in organizing. Research groups had the lowest percentage (18 percent), probably because staff are usually trained at universities and keep current through professional societies. A third of all the training budgets were under $500, but 18 percent were over $10,000.

Willingness to Use Funds and Time for Training

Four questions in The Conservation Foundation's survey measured the willingness of responding groups to pay for: a two-day training conference, a one-week conference, a one-semester course at a nearby university, and a consultant. As table 2.21 indicates, the most favored approach was the two-day conference: 63 percent of all groups would pay somewhere between $1 and $300 for it. For the other three types of training, nearly 50 percent of the groups said they would pay nothing or do not know how much they would pay. The willingness—and ability—to pay is affected by size. Among groups with memberships of 10,001 to 100,000, 89 percent would pay somewhere between $51 and $400 for a two-day session. For the week-long session, 35 percent of these groups would pay between $401 and $500 and another 24 percent would pay more; among groups with over 100,000 members, 25 percent would pay from $601 to $800 and another 25 percent would pay over $1,000 (the questionnaire options over $500 are not shown in table 2.21 because, overall, not many groups chose them). For a consultant, 33 percent of the groups with 1,001 to 10,000 members would pay $51 to $100 a day; 58 percent of the groups with between 10,001 and 100,000 members would pay from $51 to $200 a day.

Although such numbers help in indicating the priority that environmental groups place on training, several respondents commented that training is the first item to be cut from a budget. Or training may remain in the budget but fund-raising may not be sufficient to meet the budget. "Training is often regarded as gravy," according to a volunteer trainer.

Time, too, is an essential cost of training. Many respondents commented on the lack of time for training. Only 5 percent, however, said that the person in their organization who could most benefit from training would be unable to take the time to participate in a program. Three periods—one to two weeks, three to six days, or

Table 2.21

**Willingness to Pay for Training
by Percentage of Groups**

Dollars per session	Two-Day Conference	One-Week Conference	One-Semester Course	Consultant (dollars per day)
$0	14	26	28	25
$1-100	34	12	21	34
$101-200	14	9	10	11
$201-300	15	4	7	4
$301-400	6	7	4	1
$401-501	3	9	4	2
Over $501	5	9	4	2
Don't know	11	22	21	22

one or two days—are rated about equally as the time a person could be spared. Only 7 percent of the respondents thought that more than two weeks could be arranged. Smaller groups are most interested in one- to two-day programs. About 33 percent of the groups with more than 1,000 members (that is, all but the smallest groups) indicated they would send the person for three to six days. Among groups with between 10,001 to 100,000 members, 42 percent would send a person for one or two weeks.

Using internships in other organizations as a means of acquiring skills was considered "extremely useful" by 17 percent of the respondents. Another 16 percent thought such internships might be "very useful"; about 25 percent, "somewhat useful." The responses were consistent across all budget groups, except for groups with budgets between $50,001 and $100,000. In these groups, 35 percent responded that internships would be "extremely useful"; thus, fewer rated them "somewhat useful."

Attitudes toward New Institutes

As table 2.22 illustrates, the attitudes of questionnaire respondents toward a new training or policy institute are similar. A new training institute was favored by 51 percent; a new policy institute, by 59 percent. Around 25 percent of these groups strongly favored each, while about 8 percent opposed both types of new institutes.

Table 2.22

Attitudes Toward New Institutes (Percentage)

	Training	Policy
Strongly favor	23	26
Somewhat favor	28	33
Neutral	35	24
Oppose	4	6
Strongly oppose	3	2
Don't know	7	10

Perhaps the lack of strong support is best reflected in the comments of the leader of a large national group interviewed for this report: "What we really need is money to pay for specialized training that we identify as useful to our people. A new institution would be a waste of money." And another commented: "I can't see any value for us in a new institute. Our people tend to find where they need help." However, one person interviewed for this report did not share that view: "I strongly believe we need an environmental training institute for our community."

Interviews with Representatives of Environmental Groups

The various measures of training's priority for environmental groups indicate that it is of crucial importance to between 15 and 25 percent of those surveyed by The Conservation Foundation. More than 50 percent rated training an important but secondary need. If funds were available without restrictions on spending, most groups would probably spend their funds on their mission. Some minority voices, however, argued that environmental groups need to place training higher on their priority list. And the times may demand that a higher priority be given to training. Economic circumstances are resulting in more attention to management skills. The need to take part in debates and negotiations on such complex subjects as hazardous waste technologies and controls to reduce acid rain is encouraging groups to hone their policy skills on current issues.

The representatives of larger environmental groups interviewed for this report expressed many views directly and indirectly related to the questionnaire findings. On the overall need for training, some representatives said that:

- I would put the highest possible priority on training, both substantive and nuts-and-bolts management training. I have a background in industrial financial management and I am one of those very, very rare birds in conservation who knows what management is about. My board and staff have zero equipment for recognizing good management or exercising it. I am simply astonished that there is so little quality management in organizations that have become very big. This field could founder on sloppy management, poor handling of money, ineptitude that is made to look like scandals, etc.
- The environmental community desperately needs training, both in substantive issues and in management.
- There is virtually no attention given to management or management-related training. Judging by the competence and quality of what we are receiving, there is virtually no training at all going on here. It simply has no priority. In fact, we are so poorly managed that it would be hard even to assess the need for training. We have twice as much bureaucracy as we need and one-third as much management. We have a dreadfully serious and urgent need for management training.
- We find that our management people have little understanding of issues and our issues people tend to be Ph.D.s who don't even know how to manage their secretaries.
- There is a very serious need for training in my organization. Forget the issues; management is everything. People are the biggest resources and yet our budget reflects almost no provision for providing them with increasing skills as they move up. I ask myself constantly, how to deal with dysfunctional people, avoid bloodletting, put a budget together, set up a decision-making process that is efficient and also inclusive, etc. All managers in our field are at sea in so many ways.
- Training and management information resources are not being provided for in any formal or careful way. Both our board and staff are issue-oriented. We experienced real trouble in '77 and '78, had no fiscal management, and went on a roller coaster of surpluses and deficits. I am willing to try to be a manager, though that is not my background. The board has taken its responsibility much more seriously recently, and one of our trustees has said he would hire consultants to provide management advice. Fundraising, planning, image-building, and general management advice are badly needed here and in other organizations. Our budgeting and reporting processes need overhauling.

National groups felt differently about whether training in policy issues is important for staff. Some felt that their staffs already have these skills.

- The major professional groups, such as ours, which has 13 to 14 lobbyists, do not need issues expertise or training. The people hired have it already.

- The real emphasis in training should be on management. We know the issues better than anybody else. I would send lobbyists and issues people to management courses. Ultimately, the issues people will move up and run the organization, and the management we get will reflect what they know about management.

Others felt that training in the issues is needed to allow policy people an opportunity to gain additional knowledge and management people an opportunity to learn about issues.

- I wish there were much more training in substantive issue areas. I wish I knew where to go for very specialized courses in economics of environmental policies, local group organizing, how to relate to state and local governments, etc. The principal problem I have seen with short courses is that they offer little or no follow-up. After having taken a course, I would prefer to receive articles and information, synthesized materials for two years or so. This kind of program would be very useful, and we would pay for it. The core people in our key management team would need at least a week to begin. We would require a long-term and continuing updating.
- We could use some issues training in areas resisted by the staff, such as anything having to do with state and local parks. We might pay for that simply to encourage attendance and interest.
- Issues training can be helpful, but it ought to be provided on a tailored basis and preferably at a school that offers a variety of opportunities. We sent one representative to Yale, and he took courses in the Law School, the Forestry School, and the School of Organization and Management. It helped him tremendously. He has new skills, new up-to-date knowledge, new friends and contacts, and greater confidence in himself. He got his batteries charged.

There is considerable enthusiasm among larger groups for some source of information on the range and quality of training programs. Several believed that the information would best come from a group with environmental credentials.

- Information about what's available and how it is regarded could be very useful. Ideally, that could be best provided by someone or some group with environmental credentials.
- It is very hard for us to evaluate the training courses offered. The real gap is in having someone's imprimatur or stamp of approval on who does what well. A contract or on-going relationship with a national training institute might be helpful. A consumer guide to good training, or certification, or other means of verification would be highly valued, especially if it came from an environmental source we trusted.
- One could identify the handful of good consultants and make them available more broadly. I don't know who they are, but if I had a means of finding out and trusting the sources of information about them, it would be a great advantage.

- There is a great need for communication on who's doing what, where. I could sure use some training myself, but frankly wouldn't have any idea how to learn about what's available where.

As suggested earlier, little interest was generated in a new institute among the larger groups surveyed.

- A sourcebook on good training courses would be valuable to us. An institute I'm less certain is a good idea.
- A new formal program in training could be very useful to us. I question whether a new institute is necessary. I would like to know what the business schools are offering. Frankly, I don't have much sense of what's available or much idea of how to find out.
- Advanced instruction at Harvard, Duke, etc., in management for three months or so provides very useful corporate contacts for us. A new institution may be very useful to others, but it would not meet our specialized needs.

Credentials were seen as important.

- However, all you get from working is fulfillment. Therefore, credentials, a degree or certificate, could be important.
- Also, some means of acquiring credentials for our staff would be appreciated. It is always good to do something that allows you to add to your resume.

It was not clear that formal programs at educational institutions are the answer.

- There really isn't enough difference among nonprofit organizations to justify separate training efforts in management. I have not been very impressed with the academic offerings in this area. Formal graduate programs have not had much impact. In-service training is probably much more valuable and practical. I would avoid aligning with educational institutions.

One leader noted a resistance to sharing information.

- Several times I have brought up the issue of management with my counterparts in other groups and proposed that we share management successes and mistakes. They react as though I had trotted somebody's skeleton out of the closet. They all look at their hands. Nobody wants to talk about management for some reason. I wonder sometimes if I'm the only one who's having problems managing my organization. I think your project sounds like one of the most exciting and useful things I have heard of, and I would love to know what you learn from it. If there were a way to structure some training for organizations like mine, advise us where to get good training, persuade our boards that we ought to budget for it, and then find a means of sharing management information across the leadership of environmental organizations, I think those would be some of the very best services anyone could perform for the environmental movement.

Finally, some organizations were already actively involved with training.

- We run our organization like a business. The cafeteria is subsidized. Training can involve all employees. There is a constant use of short courses in data processing and other technical areas. We have implemented a management-by-objective system. Salary increases are based on merit. Evening course tuition is provided. Sabbaticals are available informally. We offer extended leave for professional people. Training is considered an important, nonmonetary benefit. Several hundred thousand dollars are spent on our annual meeting alone, which is largely training. We offer two retreats a year, using the Learning Resources Group as facilitators. We have worked hard to develop a mission statement. We also have tried to identify our strengths and weaknesses and have attempted to link our long-range plan with our budget cycle. We have professional out-placement services for separated employees. We have an employee newsletter and distribute publications to all employees. We offer an annual fall family picnic. All of this is seen as part of our overall training and morale-maintaining program. We *are* unique, though, because we are a business or corporation on a huge scale within the conservation community.
- Everybody goes to one short course or conference lasting two or three days in his or her area of specialty. Our top-tier staff of six are eligible for two weeks sabbatical per year to broaden their own knowledge of their field. One went to Africa on his own expense. The individual has to file a report. Also, a two-week river trip or park trip to the top twelve senior staff is available. The executive director gets a longer sabbatical. We think that the sabbatical program may be the best training vehicle, though we haven't had time yet to assess it. We could use some organized training in direct mail, fund-raising, etc.
- We don't budget formally for training, but we're constantly sending people to courses in data processing, direct mail fund-raising, computer training, and the like. The lawyers tend to go to specialized conferences or courses as needed. And we have sabbaticals on a case-by-case basis, paid and partly paid and unpaid. If one of our stars feels the need for some time to recharge, we work that out. It's all done informally.

To determine the need for additional training resources, the needs detailed in this chapter must be weighed against the resources already available. Some of these resources are discussed in the following chapter.

References

1. "The State of the Environmental Movement," *High Country News*, 27 May, 1983, p.1.

2. Clem L. Zinger, Richard Dalsemer, and Helen Maguire, *Environmental Volunteers in America, Findings and Recommendations of the Steering Committee of the National Center for Voluntary Action's Environmental Program*

(Prepared for the Environmental Protection Agency, 1972).

3. Allan Spader, Leonard Wilson, and Terry Bremer, *National Consultation on Local Land Conservation* (Proceedings—Interim Report, November 1981).

Chapter 3

Resources for Training

Sandra Gray Thacker, who heads the board of the North American Wolf Society, wrote to The Conservation Foundation that:

> If an organization has 350 members and a budget of approximately $2,000 per annum, it cannot afford to send anyone anywhere for training. That same organization is likely run by volunteers: volunteers who are employed full-time in an unrelated occupation, the money from which supports their volunteer interests as well as their daily survival. That type of person cannot afford time away from work to attend seminars in another part of the country, or the money to finance it.

Time, funding, distance, and lack of understanding of changing times are all obstacles to giving priority to training, particularly for smaller groups. In a response to our survey, the single staff member of a basically volunteer organization commented that older members of that organization do not recognize that environmental groups now need to address issues on a factual and economic basis, rather than by generalities, and that training is needed to do so. Distance is also a problem for groups located away from major population centers, where training is often obtained, and for those with dispersed membership and staffs.

Training needs may be met by other than formal procedures. Most training occurs on the job. In fact, this may be the most inexpensive and effective form of training. Two New Jersey organizations trained 25 new staff people through the now-defunct CETA (Comprehensive Employment Training Act) program in three years. Nineteen of the 25 are now high-level staff in nonprofit organizations, business, or government.[1] Polly Dyer, a long-time environmental leader in the state of Washington and director of continuing environmental education at the Institute for Environmental Studies at the University of Washington, stresses that volunteers work on an "each one, teach one" basis.[2] The Washington Wilderness coalition, for example, runs Washington Wilderness Weekends to train volunteers.

One respondent to The Conservation Foundation's questionnaire indicated he had no training in his speciality; rather, he read extensively and joined a network that dealt with the subject. A survey conducted by the New England Environmental Network found written materials to be the preferred method of learning in 42 out of 42 environmental issue areas and 14 of 27 leadership skill areas. A volunteer organization noted that it selects board members on the basis of professional skills, then relies on their expertise to train others. Volunteers also may develop skills through other organizations in which they are active and which can afford training programs. Larger organizations may be able to afford to hire trained people. In other cases, jobs may be so specific that training must be done in-house.

Half the groups responding to The Conservation Foundation's questionnaire did not know of resources that could meet their training needs. (Organizations with fewer than 1,000 members, without full-time staff, and with small budgets, and groups that focus on a single issue tended to know the least about how to meet their training needs.) Others indicated that advertisements for costly training programs stream across their desks, but that information about practical, inexpensive programs is much scarcer. Grass-roots groups, in particular, may question whether training programs in convention cities are relevant to those deeply involved in local controversies in rural areas. George B. Fell of the Natural Areas Association suggested in a letter to The Conservation Foundation that conferences, workshops, and courses should not dominate a training program. Rather, a clearinghouse could less expensively, in terms of both time and money, make information available to individual workers when needed. Bulletins, newsletters, journals, handbooks, bibliographies, indexes, data-base services, cassettes, and films could be run through the clearinghouse. In particular, Fell would welcome the exchange of information in areas such as personnel management, board relations, and budgeting.[4]

Environmental groups may downplay training because neither the groups nor the persons involved with them think of their work as a career. Particularly in small organizations, there is little job security, hence little reason to believe that investment in training of staff or volunteers important. Few groups have clear staff or volunteer evaluation processes. William L. Bryan, who headed the Northern Rockies Action Group for eight years, points out in an article, "Preventing Burnout in the Public Interest Community," that people in the social-change organizations with which he works seldom think in terms of a career.[5] Instead, they focus on the issue at hand. This approach is being rethought by those who entered the environmental movement around Earth Day and are now thinking about long-term goals. Career paths in environmental organizations are limited; most groups are small, and even larger groups have only a few job levels. Therefore, some staff and volunteers are thinking in terms of working in different sectors—private, government, and nonprofit—during their careers and combining their environmental interests with other skills.

Despite the obstacles, a number of environmental leaders have emphasized the need for training and urged that efforts be made to increase the skills of environmental groups. A 1972 report on environmental volunteers listed as one of six recommendations that "volunteer environmental organizations can and should work to increase the effectiveness of their organizations." The report suggested that a clearinghouse on information sources and guidance on tapping them would be useful. Over half the organizations surveyed in 1972 listed leadership development as a problem; a quarter identified it as a major problem. Many felt that environmental groups were reinventing the wheel instead of drawing on the experiences of others.[6]

Russell L. Brenneman, a conservation attorney in Hartford, Connecticut, has argued for a high degree of professionalism among land-saving organizations. In an article written in 1982, he lists training as one of six important areas in which these organizations should analyze their competence, noting that the training of volunteers and continual upgrading of their skills is often neglected. "Moreover, achieving high levels of professional competence is not an optional extra; it is essential if an organization is to survive and prosper."[7]

Bryan, in the article mentioned above, points to training programs as one way of preventing burnout among staff because:

> . . . public interest workers often don't have time to further their own skills and knowledge related to the work they are doing. This can be very frustrating because of the everchanging nature of the issues. It is easy to feel left behind and defensive about not being well informed about what you are doing. A staff development program can help alleviate this sense of frustration among staff, and at the same time, further the capabilities of the organization. We can't always be on the front lines and still be current on new developments in our field of expertise. That is why public interest groups have to have appropriate training policies. All too often, training is viewed as a frill . . .[8]

Bryan also suggests that sabbaticals be used to reward public interest workers and benefit their organizations.

Insofar as these comments and the responses to The Conservation Foundation's questionnaire suggest that there is a need for training among environmental groups—at least for some training, in some skills, among some goups—where can training be found?

Resources for training staff and members of environmental groups in the four areas described in the previous chapter—fund-raising and membership recruitment, internal management, communication and education, and policy development and research—can be found among the groups themselves; in the academic community; and in the traditional and newer types of management consulting groups or community-organizing institutes.

Training Provided by Environmental Groups

Environmental groups often train through workshops and conferences that combine sessions on communications with developing strategy on specific environmental issues. Much of this training is done on an ad hoc basis; some is done at annual meetings. A few large organizations have ongoing training projects; several small groups hold training as their primary purpose. Specialized groups offer management as well as issue training.

Some types of training are offered continually by a wide range of environmental groups, mostly to members. The Colorado Mountain Club, for example, gives courses in trekking, first aid, avalanche awareness, and backpacking as well as leadership seminars. The Maine Audubon Society runs about 100 field trips a year on subjects ranging from tidal pools to energy-efficient housing. The Virginia Forestry Association provides bus tours for landowners and co-sponsors taxation workshops. The Tennessee Environmental Council trains its members in how to work with state and local governments. National groups, both activist organizations and professional societies, provide some training through conferences and special seminars. The annual North American Wildlife and Natural Resources Conference run by the Wildlife Management Institute is one of many examples.

The most striking point about training programs offered by environmental groups may be their variety. The following six examples show the range of training approaches and give a better idea of the types of training programs available. Though all of the programs profiled aim to improve the effectiveness of environmental groups, each one originated in a different way and took an individual approach to the groups served, issues addressed, and types of training offered.

Association of New Jersey Environmental Commissions[9]

The Association of New Jersey Environmental Commissions (ANJEC) is a nonprofit, independent group created in 1969 to provide training for New Jersey's environmental commissioners. The commissioners are volunteer local officials appointed by mayors. Their responsibilities include such functions as reviewing site plans and overseeing a town's natural resource survey. ANJEC regularly sponsors a two-day course for the commissioners. The 1983 course covered pesticide use and control, water-quality monitoring, and on-site waste disposal.

ANJEC's resources are used extensively by environmental groups. In fact, ANJEC believes that training environmentalists to be professional and credible is one of its most important functions. It runs the annual New Jersey Environmental Congress, which involves government, environmental groups, and business in a day-long session of addresses, seminars, and exhibits. Special grants enable the association to offer additional courses. In 1983, for example, it provided three workshops on farmland preservation.

ANJEC publishes an annually updated handbook for commissioners and issues a quarterly technical report and various alerts and bulletins. It has a 5,000-volume library. Its staff will help members answer questions and will serve as liaison with government agencies. ANJEC is one of a half-dozen organizations chosen by the U.S. Environmental Protection Agency to provide initial access to the Chemical Substances Information Network.

ANJEC is funded primarily by foundation grants. However, a quarter of its budget, which was $160,000 in 1982, comes from dues paid by its 1,600 members. ANJEC's current staff includes five volunteers, four part-time, and four full-time paid staff.

The Land Trust Exchange[10]

The Land Trust Exchange is a national network of local private land conservation organizations. It evolved from a national conference on conserving local land sponsored by the Lincoln Institute of Land Policy in 1981. An inventory prepared for the meeting found that three-quarters of the organizations had been created since 1965. These private land conservation organizations rely heavily on volunteers;

a quarter of them have some paid staff. They are generally small; three-quarters have budgets under $20,000.

Participants in the 1981 conference felt that it was time to meet their counterparts in other groups and to try to learn tested, successful land-saving techniques from them. Some were also interested in joint political action on issues such as tax policy. Although discussed less, the need for greater attention to building management skills of the trusts was evident.

The Land Trust Exchange, now headquartered in Mount Desert, Maine, is based on the value of peer learning and support. The exchange now serves as a communication vehicle among the trusts through publications and sponsorship of meetings. Besides a directory of land trusts, the exchange publishes a quarterly journal that emphasizes tools and resources. Issues of the journal have featured program building, forming practical partnerships, setting priorities, and using computers.

A meeting sponsored by the Land Trust Exchange brought together trusts by geographical region, in this case the Midwest/Plains states. The exchange also brought land trusts together with members of the professions involved in conservation work. In one instance, a colloquium of lawyers, appraisers, and conservationists focused on valuation of easements, and their meeting resulted in plans to prepare a manual and start an experimental program to train appraisers in this speciality.

The exchange also runs a Peer Match Program for its sponsoring trusts. It matches the needs of the trusts for consulting help in various areas with people who have faced similar problems. So far, about 28 trusts serve as sponsors of the exchange. It is also supported by 300 associates and receives further funding from foundations.

New England Environmental Network[11]

The New England Environmental Network provides training for citizen leaders and staff of environmental groups in the six New England states. The network was formed in 1977 by the Lincoln Filene Center for Citizenship and Public Affairs at Tufts University with a grant from the U.S. Office of Education. Its goals are to make the best use of limited resources by encouraging cooperation among environmental and conservation groups in the region, to provide learning opportunities on issues and in management skills, and to encourage effective relations with business and industry in making environmental decisions.

The network's continuing activities include sponsorship of an annual environmental conference, publication of a quarterly newsletter, and sponsorship of a week-long environmental leadership institute. The 1983 leadership institute included sessions on fund-raising; using the media; conducting and testifying at public hearings; lobbying; forming effective partnerships with business and industry; initiating legislation and getting it through the legislative body; managing an environmental organization, using computers; networking; recruiting and using volunteers; and writing, publishing, and marketing a newsletter. About 60 people attended the one-week summer session in 1982.

Besides its regular activities, the network issues study guides on particular skills, such as using the media and writing proposals. It convenes conferences on specific issues, such as wetlands and hazardous wastes.

The network's $68,000 budget is funded now through individual donations and publication sales. Its staff of 2 full-time and 2 part-time people is supplemented by about 20 student volunteers. Training sessions offered by the network are run voluntarily by professors from Tufts or by staff or leaders of environmental groups in the region.

Nancy W. Anderson, who heads the network as director of environmental affairs for the Filene Center, cites funding as the crucial need of the network, particularly for scholarships to help reach grassroots groups.

Northern Rockies Action Group[12]

Northern Rockies Action Group (NRAG) is a training center for citizen organizations, primarily those in Idaho, Montana, and Wyoming. Its explicit goal is to build organizations to address issues that NRAG defines as progressive.

NRAG works with groups with missions to influence public policies or to educate the general public. When the group was founded 10 years ago, 80 to 90 percent of its work was with environmental groups, which now account for about 25 percent of NRAG's work. The focus has expanded to include lower-income and disarmament organizations. This shift is occurring partly because of NRAG's success. Most environmental groups in the region are now fairly sophisticated in their skills. Little call remains in the environmental community for the kinds of basic training commonly provided to newly formed organizations. The existing environmental groups have burgeoned in size and budget, and the complexity of their structure, as well as of the policy issues on which they work, has increased. NRAG's training and assistance program has been evolving to meet the much more complicated and individualized needs of the Northern Rockies' environmental community.

NRAG offers training in two broad areas—organizational skills and strategic skills. The former cover formation of an organization, management structure, planning, financial administration, public relations, and fund-raising. Strategic skills cover community organizing, media use, membership recruiting, issue strategy development, and coalition building. In the last category, for example, NRAG promotes a continuing committee of sheep producers and environmentalists. In light of the rural nature and limited resources of the groups being assisted in the Northern Rockies, NRAG consistently raises funds to subsidize its training and assistance programs, making them affordable at rates lower than actual costs.

The seven-member NRAG staff performs much of its work through on-site consultation but the staff also produces publications and conducts management workshops. NRAG may offer advice on a specific proposal or provide an entire management audit, analyzing an organization's strengths and weaknesses and suggesting means for self-improvement. NRAG publishes a series of papers that explore new strategies and techniques for citizen groups as well as various training manuals.

Sierra Club[13]

"In the mid-seventies we realized we were reinventing the wheel in areas such as how to run volunteer programs," recalls Marty Fluharty, a member of the Sierra Club's Board of Directors and chairman of Volunteer Training. Based on this realization, she prepared written materials on running volunteer programs and soon was asked by local Sierra Club chapters to come and show members how to use them.

The Grassroots Effectiveness Project grew out of this earlier training effort. It is also a response to the club's growth—147,000 of its 325,000 members have joined in the past three years. Most members do not join the Sierra Club with well-developed management or conservation skills, but they want to become active and involved. The goal of the Grassroots Effectiveness Project, then, is to provide instruction and information for training coordinators in each chapter.

The project currently focuses on the southeastern region, where two trainers are being developed for each state. These trainers, in turn, will work with leaders of Sierra groups in their home states. The subjects being dealt with include fund-raising, financial management, management of volunteer entities, strategic planning for environmental issues, negotiation, research, lobbying, campaigning, membership recruitment, and litigation. The project is run by volunteer trainers, but transportation is a major cost borne by the Sierra Club. The 1983 $12,000 budget also covered project development and materials.

The Sierra Club publishes training materials as well. An "Organizers Library" will consolidate and transmit members' experiences. So far, it includes handbooks on conservation action, election politics, grass-roots fund-raising, and volunteer leadership. An "idea" book introduces the Sierra Club structure and describes ways to build and retain membership.

The Sierra Club participates in several other types of training programs. It has trained selected volunteers to lobby in Washington. The organization also took part in 1982-83 regional conferences organized by major environmental activist groups largely in reaction to the changes in national environmental policy. The club's four-day International Assembly in the summer of 1983 provided participants a chance to attend both issue and management workshops. Recently, the club has placed increasing emphasis on the importance of training its members to participate effectively in the political process.

The Sierra Club's national headquarters in San Francisco houses a human resources development specialist, and the club provides paid staff members with orientation sessions and management training opportunities. In 1982, staff and officers from 18 chapters were brought together with the national staff in San Francisco for briefings and training sessions.

League of Women Voters of the United States/League of Women Voters Education Fund[14]

The League of Women Voters of the United States (LWVUS), although not an environmental group, is closely related to environmental groups and their training needs through its education fund. Formed in 1920, the league promotes political responsibility through informed and active participation of citizens in government.

LWVUS lobbies actively at all levels of government, but it does not support particular candidates or a particular political party. Its 113,000 members are organized into about 1,400 local leagues in all parts of the United States.

The League of Women Voters Education Fund (LWVEF) was founded as an affiliate of the league in 1957 to increase public understanding of major public-policy issues and promote awareness of options available in government decision making. The LWVEF provides training for the general public and for members of local leagues on a variety of issues through conferences, publications, and technical assistance.

Since the fund's inception, natural resources have been an important part of its work. The education fund originally focused on water issues. By 1982, the natural resources department of the fund was involved in a range of energy issues as well as air, water, and land use. Funds for LWVEF now come from foundations, corporate and individual contributions, and publication sales. Earlier, some funding came from the federal government.

The current three-year project on hazardous waste management policy illustrates the way in which the fund operates. The program's goal is to "empower citizens with the substantive facts, the procedural know-how and the financial backing necessary to be effective in their communities on hazardous waste issues." During the first year, an advisory committee was established, league members were informed about the project, a clearinghouse and roster of experts were organized, and pass-through grants were made to local leagues for specific projects. In addition, a study guide, a bibliography, an audiovisual catalog, and a newsletter were developed. Specific projects are now being undertaken by 20 local leagues. Training takes place not only through publications and conferences but also through daily contacts that the four natural resources staffers in the LWVEF have with local league members. Isabelle Weber, director of natural resources for the education fund, estimates she and her staff of three spend between a third and half of their time on such contacts.

The league's training is not limited to policy issues. Training in membership recruitment is currently a major emphasis. Except for 1976, when the league sponsored presidential debates, membership had declined about 5,500 a year during the 1970s. A national recruitment campaign resulted in a net gain of 7,200 members in 1982. A major training project has been part of the campaign.

The league also uses training to deal with other changes. Turnover of members is increasing, and members now spread their skills over more responsibilities. In response, the board and staff are offering more training. One way of meeting the need is to involve all members of the LWVUS and LWVEF staff in training, says Nancy Robberson, director of management and training services. She has four training specialists on her staff. Workshops on burnout and stress management have been held. The staff also prepares guides to program planning and facilitates exchange of information among chapters on programs that have worked.

Summary

The six organizations with training efforts just discussed share some characteristics. Except for the League of Women Voters, the groups are young—between 1 and 14 years old. They emerged with the environmental movement. Their training budgets are fairly small. All but the Sierra Club project have paid staff, but none has more than eight.

Volunteers, therefore, play an important role. They run the Sierra Club project. Profesors and students often work as volunteers for the New England Environmental Network. Much of the Land Trust Exchange's work is carried out through volunteer peer exchange. Five of ANJEC's 13-member staff are volunteers. Although the LVWUS now relies more on paid staff, it remains primarily a volunteer group.

All six of the training groups limit their focus in geographical area, subject addressed, or types of groups served. Two operate in a region, one in a state, and three nationally.

The modes of delivering training differ mainly in emphasis. ANJEC and the Land Trust Exchange perform clearinghouse functions, but like the other groups also operate through workshops of varying lengths. NRAG offers more specific types of consulting services than the others. ANJEC specializes in substantive issues. The others cover the entire range of training needs, with NRAG concentrating on organizational and strategy assistance and the Sierra Club (in its Grassroots Effectiveness Project), on organizational skills.

Interest in running organizations as efficiently as possible is reflected in the new emphasis on management training in groups such as the Sierra Club. The National Volunteer Project of the Appalachian Mountain Club has just released a bibliography to aid groups concerned about program planning, fund-raising, membership development, and other organizational and technical skills.

The Land Trust Exchange is not the only organization trying to help groups learn from one another. The Environmental Action Foundation runs a matching program on waste issues; it helps fund the travel of a member from a group that has experience with a problem to consult with another group facing a similar problem. A natural resources swap shop is featured in the League of Women Voters Prospectus to help local affiliates learn from each other.

There appear to be two major needs to which training offered by environmental groups themselves does not now respond. Except for NRAG, the groups provide very limited management training of the kind helpful to the staff of medium-sized and large environmental groups. Accord, a conflict-management training group in Boulder, Colorado, has provided internal management training for one large environmental group.

A second area of major need is in training for research and policy development. As discussed later in this chapter, during the 1970s millions of federal government dollars went into educating environmental groups and their constituencies about environmental issues. While little of this support went directly to training in research or policy development techniques, it did enable environmental groups to inform themselves and others about the basic factors involved in key environmental issues. Federal funds now have been drastically cut, and only a small proportion has been replaced with funds from other sources, although environmental issues grow more complicated.

Training Provided by Other Organizations

Training has been a growth industry for a number of years. Associations, universities (particularly in continuing education units), consultants, peer networks, and publishers offer a myriad of courses, seminars, workshops, books and journals, and films and audiocassettes on training in many skills. A number of institutions have served corporate and public agencies for several decades. Several of the environmental groups that responded to our training questionnaire rely on these institutions.

Traditional Institutions

Many traditional institutions are involved in training (usually referred to in the literature as "human resource development"). The efforts of these institutions are not directed specifically toward the training needs of environmenal groups, or, for the most part, even toward nonprofit groups in general. Nonetheless, environmental groups may be able to apply these resources to some of their particular training needs.

Publications. The 955-page *Training and Development Organizations Directory*[15] is a basic reference book describing 1,967 individuals and organizations that offer training. *Training*[16], a monthly journal that reports on all aspects of training and sponsors an annual conference, reaches 42,000 subscribers and serves to help trainers keep current on trends in the field.

Ronald Press, a division of John Wiley & Sons, and Prentice-Hall, Inc., are two of the many publishers that generate training materials and texts. Addison-Wesley Publishing Company offers a separate "Human Resource Development" book catalog, listing about 200 current titles. The Bureau of National Affairs has launched a new subsidiary, BNA Communications, Inc., which offers workshops and guidebooks.

Given the diversity of training resources, efforts to categorize, organize, and target them to specific nonprofit sectors are quite useful. One such effort, funded by the Edna McConnell Clark Foundation and the Exxon Education Foundation, led to the 1982 publication *The Resource Directory for Funding and Managing Nonprofit Organizations*, compiled by Ann M. Heywood.[17] Although most of this 83-page booklet is devoted to aspects of fund-raising, the last chapter, "Making the Most of the Money: Publications and Organizations Providing Technical Assistance," attempts, modestly, to categorize the vast array of available resources. The membership directory of the Nonprofit Management Association,[18] to be published sometime in 1984, will also fill a need for compiling training sources; a geographical index and annotations of each member's capabilities are to be included. Publications on fund-raising and management are available from the Foundation Center,[19] the Public Service Materials Center,[20] the Public Management Institute,[21] and the Taft Corporation.[22]

American Society for Training and Development (ASTD).[23] ASTD, established in 1947 and located in Washington, D.C., has 22,000 members who pay annual dues of $80 each and is the only organization in the United States dedicated to serving the needs of the training professional. With 120 chapters in 9 geographic regions, the association has 6 divisions and 46 special interest groups, and delivers 14 membership services. These services include the monthly *Training and Development Journal*, access to a resource center for problem solving, a placement referral service, several networking tools (such as a membership directory, *Who's Who in Training and Development*, and a voluntary computerized network of specialists willing to share expertise), a national conference, and an extensive publications program.

American Management Association (AMA)[24]. The AMA was founded in 1923 and now has five regional offices. It is the world's largest management education organization, with 90,000 members each paying annual dues of $110. The AMA's extensive programs and services are provided to over 150,000 private- and public-sector managers a year. Its top-of-the-line training program, targeted mainly to business executives, is a $2,400 management course given in four one-week units. Other special programs include courses on "Executive Effectiveness" and "Improving Management Skills of the New or Prospective Manager." The AMA's catalog for March-October 1983 lists more than 260 separate courses, some repeated many times in different locations. These courses range from "Corporate Planning" to "Human Resource and Personnel Issues" to "Sales and Marketing," "Finance and Accounting," "Risk Management," "Information Systems," and "Administrative Operations." In addition, the AMA offers tailored, on-site training programs.

American Society of Association Executives (ASAE).[25] Founded in 1920, ASAE is dedicated to enhancing the professionalism of association executives, to improving the performance of voluntary membership organizations, and to assisting associations in dealing with public policy issues. In responses to The Conservation Foundation's questionnaire, professional societies headquartered in Washington frequently mentioned using ASAE services. The membership includes more than 10,000 individual executives, each paying annual dues of $125, from trade associations, professional societies, and other not-for-profit voluntary membership organizations. Membership in ASAE, which has affiliated local chapters, offers access to over 175 professional development and education seminars and workshops, two annual conferences, publications—including the journal *Association Management*—and an executive employment clearinghouse. In addition, ASAE can provide a three-day evaluation of the strengths and weaknesses of a member's association. Members have access to "Information Central," a resource center of 2,000 volumes and 30,000 files, staffed by information specialists who respond to requests for information on all aspects of association management.

National Training Laboratories (NTL), Institute for Applied Behavioral Science.[26] NTL teaches leadership development to organization and community leaders. The approximately 150 programs presented by NTL each year, usually offered in 5-, 6-, 9-, and 11-day formats, deal with a variety of subjects in management training, training of trainers, and training for consultants on organizational development. NTL, founded in 1947, was reorganized in 1975 as a professional member organization with members chosen from a pool of more than 350 behavioral scientists in the United States and abroad. Corporations, government agencies, and voluntary associations use NTL services.

Universities. Universities offer training courses, courses to train potential trainers (for example, the Georgetown University Training Development Specialist Certificate program), and a vast variety of management courses, often in traditional business schools. Special institutes or courses for nonprofit groups can be found at many graduate business schools and schools of public administration. Robert F. Leduc of the Anschutz Family Foundation has prepared a list of 113 institutions of formal education that provide training in nonprofit organization management.[27] The list is a national survey and includes the names of the appropriate professors to be contacted. Because it does not include any information on specific courses, however, some follow-up would be required to determine how many of these programs can fulfill the needs of environmental groups.

In addition, more than 50 universities across the United States offer short courses in executive development designed for corporate executives. The Pennsylvania State University, which offers extensive development programs through the College of Business Administration, recently conducted its third annual survey of executive education. Among the Fortune 500 companies, 86 percent sponsor top-level executives in campus-based programs of at least two weeks duration; many send upper-middle managers as well.[28] Although in-house training programs can be tailored to the specific needs of organizations and afford savings in both time and money, on-campus education gives a chance to obtain a broader perspective and outside contacts. The institutions most frequently cited in the Penn State survey as providers of quality executive education include Harvard, Stanford, Columbia, Massachusetts Institute of Technology, and, not surprisingly, Pennsylvania State University.

Some executives from environmental organizations interviewed for this report expressed an interest in this type of on-campus program.

One program geared specifically to nonprofit and association managers is sponsored by the American Society of Association Executives and is run through the University of Maryland College of Business and Management. The certificate program costs $1,800 and includes 225 classroom hours, presented in 9 units.

Volunteer: National Center for Citizen Involvement.[29] With headquarters in Boulder, Colorado, and Arlington, Virginia, Volunteer: National Center for Citizen Involvement is an organization dedicated to improving volunteerism. The center has a resource library and book distribution service; it sponsors leadership development conferences and training institutes.

United Way.[30] Local United Way agencies, traditionally reacting to community needs and existing to serve them, are becoming a source of training for nonmember agencies in some management areas. Over 100 local United Way agencies now have "management assistance programs," offering training workshops or consultations to both member and nonmember groups in their communities.

The Grantsmanship Center[31]

Because the more traditional training institutions like the American Management Association and the American Society of Association Executives are generally expensive, a new organization, the Grantsmanship Center, emerged to meet the training needs of nonprofit groups that flourished as an outgrowth of the social programs of the 1960s. Founded in 1973 in Los Angeles, the Grantsmanship Center has been described as a "benevolent consulting firm."[32]

The *Grantsmanship Center News*, started in 1972, is a bi-monthly journal addressing specifically the management concerns of nonprofit organizations. With 13,000 subscribers, the journal focuses on planning programs and translating project goals into funding proposals. Special reprint packages are available. For under $20 each, a basic "Grantsmanship Information Package," a "Finance and Management Package," a "Fund-Raising and Nonprofit Support Package," and a "Personnel Management Package" can be bought.

The center has engaged in policy research to address critical issues of philanthropy, in advocacy for more effective public and private information systems about funding, in services for the alumni of its programs, and in training or technical assistance programs. Currently the center offers three different week-long training programs in 20 different cities at a cost of $395 each. The basic grantsmanship course covers proposal writing, program planning, and the changing nature of government, foundation, and corporate funding. The fund-raising course includes planning a campaign, locating prospects, donors and volunteers, and developing techniques and strategies. The program management course covers management by objective, management styles, use of financial systems, and evaluation techniques.

In addition, the center offers an intensive three-day workshop (for $275) on foundation and corporate grants, keyed to organizations that are trying to find fund-raising sources other than the government. Other special programs include a "Board Development Workshop," tailored and in-house training, or consulting arrangements to help in such areas as organizational problem solving, organizational development, and conflict resolution.

In the March/April 1983 issue of the *Grantsmanship Center News*, the center announced it will no longer be a nonprofit organization competing with other nonprofits for grant support. Rather, it will become an unconventional, privately owned corporation and will likely begin to offer certain programs to the business community. Revenues generated from these services would subsidize services to nonprofits. In the past, nonprofit organizations' attendance at workshops has been subsidized, in part, by foundation grants.

Management Support Organizations

Management support organizations (MSOs) are a group of relatively new institutions that provide management training to nonprofit groups. MSOs have been used already by some environmental organizations and probably could be used by even more.

In the words of Clarke Maylone, former executive director of the Nonprofit Management Association, a group with over 230 members, MSOs, which provide "joint consultant/client problem solving and in-service transfer of skills and information, were created in the 1970s to meet a variety of technical assistance needs. There is a healthy diversity among MSOs with respect to concerns, specialities, client focuses and modes of operations."[33] However, according to Maylone, several generalities apply to the majority of MSOs.

- They are nonprofit organizations.
- They serve small and medium-sized nonprofits.
- They provide a mix of services, typically including training workshops, one-to-one assistance, and regular or occasional printed material.
- Their service fees are charged on a sliding-scale, ability-to-pay basis, ranging from zero to less than commercial rates.

- Their income derives from a combination of fees and third-party grants or contracts, from government or private sources.
- Their small staffs are supplemented by on-call associates and by volunteers from the public and private sectors.
- They value follow-through support and encourage self-help. Most providers have a local or state base of operations.

Typically small and flexible, MSOs reflect the philosophies and visions of their founders. They are located in cities across the country. Some examples include: the Center for Community Change and the Management Assistance Group (Washington, D.C., New York, and California); the Community Technical Assistance Center (Pittsburgh); Center for Management Assistance (Kansas City); the Technical Assistance Center (Denver); and Community Training and Development (San Francisco).[34]

The Support Center.[35] Founded in 1973, the Support Center is one of the oldest and best known of the MSOs. It is staffed by 20 people but also draws on the resources of professors, volunteers (for instance, experts from the big-eight accounting firms), and students. Offices are located in San Francisco, Washington, D.C., Chicago, Newark, Houston, and Oklahoma City. The center specializes in planning and organizational development, budget and accounting systems, and fund-raising. In 1983, it provided support to over 500 diverse organizations. Not ideologically motivated, the Support Center's operation is funded by a mix of foundation and corporate grants and fees for services. Typically, its clients are small to medium-sized organizations with budgets from $20,000 to $1 million.

The Youth Project.[36] A nonprofit public foundation started in 1972, the Youth Project is committed to bringing about long-term positive social change and to the development of democratic citizen participation. It has five regional offices—New York, San Francisco, Minneapolis, Knoxville, Tennessee, and Atlanta. The project provides modest seed grants to local groups that encourage grass-roots activism, sponsors workshops and training sessions on grass-roots fund-raising, and offers other technical assistance on legal, financial, and management issues. In addition, the center promotes networking and serves as a broker for foundation donors.

Community Training and Development (CTD).[37] CTD began in 1976 as a community service project of the Golden Gate chapter of the American Society for Training and Development (ASTD). A nonprofit organization, CTD draws on the consulting services of 250 volunteers and provides management assistance to other Bay Area nonprofit groups through workshops and direct consulting. CTD's total expenditures for 1982-83 were $127,000, 30 percent funded by revenues from the workshop series and 70 percent funded by grants.

Up to 120 days of management training workshops are offered in a comprehensive fall and spring series. Topics covered include board development, budget preparation, writing skills, public relations, conference planning, and negotiation. The workshops are conducted in four Bay Area locations and serve approximately 2,400 people a year, representing 600 to 700 organizations from nine Bay Area counties. Each workshop lasts one or two days and costs about $30.

The CTD volunteer consulting service is offered on a client-initiated basis to organizations with an annual operating budget of under $400,000. In the 1982-83 period, 65 clients sought services on information systems, financial management, board skills, fund-raising, organizational structure, by-laws, planning, goal definition, membership development, and other topics. In a typical case handled by CTD, less than 6 hours of CTD time is needed for initial consultation, and then about 50 hours is donated by a professional working on the case.

A new executive development program is being offered as an extension of the CTD service. The six program elements include:

- small problem-solving groups (six to nine participants from comparable organizations) that meet over several months for mutual assistance;
- scholarships for participating agency directors who need them;
- high-quality training that addresses such sensitive issues as program duplication;
- guest status for participating agency directors at several corporate training programs;
- a roundtable to share ideas and promote joint ventures; and
- the opportunity to learn from managers in other organizations.

Six other organizations in the Bay Area—the Support Center, the Management Center, the Executive Service Corps, RSVP (Retired Senior Volunteer Project), United Way Assistance, Volunteer, and the Junior League Assistance Project—offer services similar to those provided by CTD.[38] (Although Harbinger Communications, 50 Rustic Lane, Santa Cruz, Calif., is not an MSO, it is noteworthy as a nonprofit organization that delivers training in information management, made possible through the efficient use of computers. Harbinger assists 18 nonprofits in the Monterey/San Francisco Bay areas in managing their membership and financial information. The director encourages groups to acquire microcomputers to enable them to use the SPIRES Service, a cheap, public access service provided by the Stanford Computer Center.)

Since 1974, there have been annual national conferences of MSOs. The Support Center, a recognized leader in the field, often serves as host for these conferences, which have sought to define operations, to delineate the technical assistance most needed by clients, and to understand who these clients are or might be. The Stone, Medina Johnson, Mott, Weyerhauser Company, McDonald, and many other foundations have all supported the MSO concept and development process. The Mott Foundation, for example, funded a study, *Resources and Strategies for Improving the Management of Nonprofit Organizations*, which was conducted in 1979 by the Support Center with the assistance of the Nonprofit Resource Institute. The report recommended that foundations and corporations increase their funding of activities that would lead to better management of nonprofit organizations.[39]

Certain trends seem to indicate that a consolidation and maturation in the MSO field is taking place. The Nonprofit Management Association hosted a ninth National Conference on Nonprofit Management and Technical Assistance in June 1983 and is publishing an updated directory of approximately 230 members. It is becoming clear that MSOs need to develop some kind of collaborative system for advertising and selling their programs and some standards for accreditation. Moreover, because of funding competition, some MSOs may merge with or become affiliated with for-profit management consulting or accounting firms.

Community-Organizing Training Centers

Centers that train community organizers have been particularly active in helping these leaders deal with local environmental problems, such as hazardous waste sites or exposure to toxic substances in the workplace. The role of the community organizer is catalytic—to bring people together, to identify and research the rallying issue or issues, and to develop strategies for creating change.

Some centers have a long history of training organizers in the skills necessary to take part in the democratic process. The Highlander Center in New Market, Tennessee, just celebrated its 50th anniversary of service to Appalachia and the South. Its current work includes providing opportunities for local representatives to come together to learn how to gather information about occupational and environmental health problems and how to take action based on this research, such as presenting findings to state environmental offices.

The civil rights and antiwar movements and community action agency efforts fueled a rapid expansion of grass-roots community-organizing programs throughout the 1970s. For example, a 1980 issue of *Community Jobs* listed 11 training schools, 9 of which offered regularly scheduled organizer training programs. All offered workshops on membership recruitment, leadership development strategy and tactics, research, fund-raising, and media skills. The schools differ in that some place more emphasis on "nuts-and-bolts" skills such as knocking on doors and running meetings, whereas others emphasize analytical skills such as identifying how problems affect individuals and identifying power relationships in a community. Some of these schools are primarily local or regional in orientation. Others work with state or multistate organizers.

An unusual statewide effort, housed at the University of Massachusetts at Amherst, is the Citizen Involvement Training Project (CITP).[40] Dedicated to the New England tradition of direct democracy through the town meeting process, CITP was founded in 1976 as a collaborative project of the Division of Continuing Education and Cooperative Extension Service, supported by a grant from the W.K. Kellogg Foundation. The original staff of 11 published a set of eight citizen training manuals—guides on how to use the political process, how to use the media, planning program development, and so on—geared to helping local citizen groups throughout Massachusetts. This constituency was made up of neighborhood groups, cooperatives, senior citizens, and youth groups as well as departments of state government and national organizations such as the Solar Lobby. Now, with a second three-year grant from Kellogg, CITP is providing training and technical assistance to community development corporations to help citizens undertake community economic initiatives.

Two groups working in this tradition, mainly on environmental issues, are the *Urban Environment Conference*[41] and the *Citizens Clearinghouse for Hazardous Waste*[42]. The Urban Environment Conference (UEC) was founded in 1971 to link labor and minority groups with environmental organizations. Through its five-year-old Occupational Health and Education Center for Minorities, UEC has provided at least two hours of training for over 2,000 workers and reached another 16,000 with materials appropriate to their jobs and languages. UEC organized a national leadership institute for minorities in 1983 that brought together several hundred minority leaders, labor and community organizers, and environmental and health professionals to share information and skills.

The Citizen's Clearinghouse for Hazardous Wastes grew out of the experience of its president, Lois Gibbs, in organizing her neighbors to deal with Love Canal. The national group provides training for local leaders concerned about hazardous waste problems. For example, the clearinghouse will help a group master media relations and fund-raising; it also teaches how to locate and interpret technical information.

Graduate Environmental Studies Programs as a Training Resource

There are 92 graduate-level environmental studies programs in the United States.[43] These programs are diverse; the term environmental studies carries no universally accepted program connotations. Some of the older programs are rooted in a particular discipline or skill (forestry, for example), whereas the newer programs often grew out of interdisciplinary, policy-based orientations. Most large institutions have a variety of programs or courses that relate to environmental resource management. Those responsible for these programs or courses on any one campus may or may not talk to one another. And the students are not preparing for one, clearly defined profession. However, a fledgling professional association, founded in 1975 and with a current membership of 750, the National Association of Environmental Professionals, is attempting to give more credibility to the environmental studies degree.

In late June 1983, The Conservation Foundation hosted a small, informal one-day meeting with representatives from foundations and various graduate programs in environmental studies. The purpose of this meeting was to discuss the status of the graduate programs in general and to explore how these programs provide training for environmental groups in particular. At the meeting, it was generally agreed that the programs were at some sort of crossroad. The diversity of approaches in teaching environmental studies, the general lack of clarity over the type of professional to be produced, and a declining interest in environmentalism contribute to the need for reassessing what is wanted and what is needed.

Environmental Studies Programs at a Crossroad

The underlying problem facing the graduate programs is to define the purposes they are intended to serve. Because environmental studies is not a clearly defined discipline, it is difficult to develop or justify "environmental studies" research. Likewise, it is difficult to rationalize the environmental studies degree as a professional degree because there is no specific profession to which it leads. The jobs in which environmental studies graduates have been placed are diverse, and in many cases it is not clear that training in a particular discipline, supplemented by some other courses, would not have prepared the student better for a career working on environmental issues.

The questions of purpose and identification have become more obvious and pressing because of the difficulties the graduate programs now face. Not only are there fewer students enrolled in many of the programs, but the quality of those students has also declined. Tight university budgets pressure the programs to cut back expenditures and to assume responsibility for raising funds. Job placement for graduates of the programs is increasingly difficult, especially during times of economic uncertainty and sharp reductions in government domestic spending.

The problems of self-identification must be answered in an even broader context. What is the responsibility and the capability of universities to respond to social problems, whether these problems be urban blight, treatment of blacks and women, or environmental threats? The now-recognized profession of city planning grew out of an attempt to deal with urban problems, and environmental studies may evolve similarly. "Business administration" is no more a discipline or route to a specific job description than "environmental studies." Yet schools of business administration are thriving, and the job market for students graduating with MBAs is much clearer.

The problems of enrollment, funding, and job placement require that environmental studies programs recognize the social context in which they operate. Better links are needed with industry, government, and the nonprofit sector. Many of the schools do not have even an advisory committee to establish such links. Within the university, the relationships of the programs with other disciplines and other professional schools need to be examined and the possibility of cooperative efforts explored. And, finally, the programs in different universities need to develop forms of cooperation. Little communication among them exists at present.

Profiles of Some Graduate Environmental Studies Programs

The environmental studies programs at Duke University, the University of California at Los Angeles (UCLA), and the University of Michigan illustrate the diversity of such programs.

Duke. Founded during the 1930s, the School of Forestry and Environmental Studies at Duke University has revised its programmatic structure over the years. Currently, the school offers the following degree tracks: Forest Management Science, Forest Productivity, Water and Air Resources, Resource Economics and Policy, Natural Resource Ecology, and Ecotoxicology.

Duke's School of Forestry and Environmental Studies has a resident faculty of 20 and a student body of 150. About 100 students are candidates for either the M.F. (Master of Forestry) or the M.E.M. (Master of Environmental Management); the balance are Ph.D candidates. Students planning careers in teaching and research are urged to follow a course of study leading to the Ph.D.

The School of Forestry and Environmental Studies was one of the first to recognize the importance of policy analysis in forestry and natural resources. With a grant from the Andrew W. Mellon Foundation in 1978, the Center for Resource and Environmental Policy Use was established at Duke as a flexible, multidisciplinary unit, drawing mainly on faculty from the School of Forestry and Environmental Studies. The center maintains strong ties to the schools of Law, Business Administration, and Engineering and to the Institute of Policy Sciences and Public Affairs. It also maintains close ties with officials from government and industry and with faculty and students at other institutions, particularly those nearby, such as the University of North Carolina at Chapel Hill. The center has a broad research program addressing resource-environmental problems.

Four years ago, Duke launched its Senior Professional Program in the School of Forestry and Environmental Studies. It is designed to attract into a master's program about 10 professionals a year who have 10 to 15 years work experience in resource agencies. Although the primary emphasis of this program is to analyze forestry investment opportunities in the Southeast, attention is also paid to other topics—for example, the international forest-products market.

UCLA. The UCLA program leading to the degree of Doctor of Environmental Science and Engineering (D.Env.) started in 1969.

It was conceived to use the resources of the university to help the state of California improve its air quality. The basis of the program was an applied interdisciplinary curriculum substantially different from conventional Ph.D. programs.

Formal entry into the program now requires a master's degree in a field within the natural sciences, engineering, or public health. In the four-year doctoral program, students take additional courses in areas outside their specialities, spend a year as a member of an interdisciplinary research team, take a series of written and oral exams, and spend several periods as paid interns at outside institutions where they gain applied research experience under guidance. In the past, the program has had about 16 entrants and graduates a year.

The program at UCLA is no longer a free-standing interdepartmental program; rather, it now has a rotating chairman reporting to the School of Public Health. Richard Perrine, one of the founders of the UCLA program, notes that wide acceptance of applied research and innovative education is still a problem, even when a program, like UCLA's, is successful: "Where do we place the balance point in a choice between education at the doctoral level designed to meet the needs of society and education that most conveniently adapts to the needs . . . of university faculty?"[44]

University of Michigan. The University of Michigan School of Natural Resources offers programs at the bachelor's, master's, and doctoral levels to accommodate students who want a liberal education, a professional education, or a research-science education. There are five basic programs at the graduate level: Environment and Behavior; Forest Resources; Ecology, Fisheries, and Wildlife; Landscape Architecture; and Resource Policy and Management. The school awards a Master of Science in Natural Resources (M.S.N.R.), Master of Forestry (M.F.), Master of Landscape Architecture (M.L.A.), and Master of Regional Planning (M.R.P.), as well as the Ph.D. In addition, there are interdepartmental master's degrees in water resource management and science and concurrent master's degrees in natural resource policy and law or business administration. Furthermore, there are training, research, and teaching opportunities provided by the project for the study of natural resource and environmental conflict.

The School of Natural Resources is currently restructuring its program in response to a university request that the school cut its budget by 33 percent. A university committee recommended that the school boost its doctoral program, increase its disciplinary research effort, reduce the number of master's and undergraduate students, and reorganize its curriculum. The faculty of the school argues that a 20 percent budget cut would be the largest that could be sustained and disagrees with the university committee's recommendations. Many professors point out that the job market for graduates with doctorates is very limited but that the professional training and applied focus of a master's degree is in demand. Furthermore, the faculty believes that a retreat from integrative and applied research and professional training diminishes the breadth and uniqueness of the school's educational mission. The outcome of this debate over the viability of the University of Michigan's environmental studies program should provide valuable insights for the future direction of similar programs.

Internships and Fellowships

At UCLA, internships are a key component of the doctoral program; voluntary and paid internships at the master's level may be harder to arrange. At the Yale School of Forestry, the Richard King Mellon Summer Internships for students constitute an important aspect of the total program.

The Center for Environmental Intern Programs (CEIP), with offices in Boston, San Francisco, Cleveland, and Seattle, serves as a clearinghouse that matches internship opportunities with interested students.[45] The internships offer short-term paid professional opportunities—in government, nonprofit institutions, and corporations—for upper-level undergraduate and graduate students interested in environmentally related fields. CEIP placed interns in over 1,500 projects between 1972 and 1981. Table 3.1 shows the range of CEIP's internship placements.*

Fellowships for mid-career training are available through the Richard King Mellon Foundation at the Yale School of Forestry and Environmental Science. The program aims at various types of pro-

---

* Matching graduates to jobs is an even more difficult task. *Environmental Opportunities*, a subscription newsletter published by Sanford Berry and sponsored by the Environmental Studies Department, Antioch/New England Graduate School, Keene, New Hampshire, is an attempt to fill this vacuum. Some local networks, such as the Metropolitan Washington Environmental Professionals, hold meetings in which graduates seeking jobs may mingle with prospective employers and discover leads. These networks also publish newsletters that include job/internship announcement columns.

Table 3.1

Distribution of Environmental Intern Project Listings by Discipline and Application Area Groups

(Compiled from 1,485 project listings provided by
The Center for Environmental Intern Programs, Boston, Massachusetts, 1981)

	Administration Planning, and Regulation	Resource Management	Quantitative Methods	Education	Instrumentation and Technology	Health Affairs	Total
Social Sciences	128	46	42	75	1	8	300
Biological Sciences	13	74	86	79	19	2	273
Business Administration	103	25	38	9	18	4	197
Engineering	37	26	23	8	66	14	174
Law	134	22	4	1	3	3	167
Natural Resources	28	46	49	22	5	0	150
Physical Sciences	15	13	19	5	45	8	105
Architecture	30	32	1	6	6	1	76
Transportation	29	1	11	1	1	0	43
Total	517	285	273	206	164	40	1,485

Source: R. Rajagopal, "Environmental Internships: Where are They and Who is Wanted?," Panel Resource Paper #1, Peer Assistance Network in Experiential Learning, National Society for Internships and Experiential Education, Raleigh NC 27605.

fessionals in nonprofit natural resource and environmental organizations—the young person who needs further training to pursue his or her career, the person near the end of a career who wants to crystallize his or her experience, and those who want to pursue a specific training goal or who have a specific project on which to work. Plans call for a minimum of 10 fellowships to be awarded in a five-year period.

There are other programs not attached to universities. The German Marshall Fund[46] offers internships for U.S. environmentalists in cooperation with the Institute for European Environmental Policy. About 8 staff members of nonprofit environmental groups have been among the 20 interns selected to spend two months or so in Europe under this program. The goal is to enhance the professional development of Americans by exposing them to European policy-making and policy implementation processes.

Another fellowship program, aimed broadly at public affairs training but available to professionals with environmental interests, is administered by the Coro Foundation.[47] Twelve fellows are selected annually on the basis of their demonstrated potential for public leadership. The program entails nine months of full-time training by a rotating internship in government, business, labor, the media, and political and community organizations. Graduates of the program may obtain a master's degree in Public Policy Analysis from the Claremont Graduate School after completion of a summer's residency and thesis requirement at Claremont.

The Kellogg National Fellowship Program[48] annually selects 50 young persons from academic, business, government, and other professional areas to receive as much as $30,000 over three years to work on a nondegree, self-directed plan of study. The Kellogg Foundation believes there is a crucial need to foster the development of individuals whose knowledge cuts across traditional specialities. The fellowships are designed to lead to new skills, competencies, and levels of understanding necessary to develop the broadly oriented perspectives needed to deal with social issues. Fellows have been selected from the fields of health, the sciences and social sciences, agriculture, education, business, and law. A condition of acceptance of the fellowship award is that the employing institution or agency allow the fellow at least 25 percent released time from his or her job to allow for work on a self-directed project.

Participation in campus public interest research groups (PIRGs) is another way for students (primarily undergraduates) to obtain broader experience and develop their skills. Operating in over two dozen states and Canada, PIRGs are student-funded and controlled but professionally staffed. They offer students a chance to participate in citizen/consumer advocacy organizations and to gain practical experience in dealing with public officials and the media. New York PIRG students and organizers have published three major reports on toxic pollution in New York State and have helped Love Canal residents deal with state and local government.

Environmental Studies Programs as
Training Grounds for Environmental Groups

In responses to The Conservation Foundation questionnaire, university environmental studies programs were mentioned only rarely as training resources for environmental groups. The connection is fairly indirect; the majority of graduates from these programs seek employment with government, industry, or consulting firms. There are probably not enough environmental organizations to warrant tailoring more than one or two environmental studies programs to them. Training in management skills probably can be obtained adequately in university business and public administration programs, as described earlier in this chapter.

Substantive policy issues and methods of policy analysis are addressed in environmental studies programs, but there are impediments to offering this training, beyond the confines of these programs, to staff or volunteers in environmental groups. It is difficult to hire faculty, already committed to an 11-month program, to take on additional short courses. Proper market research for such courses is also difficult. However, a regionally oriented short course, "Decisions for the Great Lakes," has been offered successfully to a broad audience through the Environmental Studies Center at the State University of New York at Buffalo. The University of Vermont is planning several citizen-oriented conferences for next year—a symposium on transport questions associated with acid rain and a meeting highlighting forestry research efforts of selected women scientists. The Yale School of Forestry and Environmental Studies sponsors a series of lectures and symposia on policy topics. And *Environmental Literature*, the new bibliography published by the school, is a promising service that will help alert the environmental community to new policy publications. This sort of activity will help to tie universities more directly to environmental groups.

Funding Sources for Training

Several potential funding sources for training environmental groups are available: government, industry, private philanthropic foundations, and the resources of the environmental groups themselves.

Chapter 2 discussed the amount of money that environmental groups in The Conservation Foundation's survey were willing to pay for various types of training and also the amount of money currently budgeted for training. The budgeted amount significantly underestimates what the groups actually pay for training because many forms of training are not separately identified or budgeted. Nevertheless, given the very limited resources of most environmental groups, outside funding is clearly necessary for many kinds of training.

Government Support

During the 1970s, the U.S. Environmental Protection Agency (EPA) spent several million dollars on training projects run by environmental and other groups. These grants were often made under citizen participation programs in various EPA offices. Grants for training also came from other agencies, such as the U.S. Department of Education and the Occupational Safety and Health Administration. Generally, these grants enabled staff and leaders of environmental groups, whether paid or volunteer, to learn about an issue and then to educate their constituency and the broader public. The goal of the grant programs was to develop broader and more informed participation in decisions on environmental policy.

One of the first grants EPA made for training citizen groups went to the Better Air Coalition to support a workshop on air-quality issues. This was followed in 1972 by a $10,000 grant to the same Baltimore group to train three student interns in air pollution abatement. Marsha Ramsay, who set up and ran the Better Air Coalition program, recalls that she used university and other community resources to provide the interns with training in the scientific, legal, and policy aspects of air pollution control and taught the community-organizing component herself.

Also during the 1970s, The Conservation Foundation organized a series of training programs by Clem Rastatter. The programs, funded by federal agencies, were opportunities for members of environmental and other citizen groups, as well as state and local government officials, to learn skills and obtain the information needed to take part in key environmental policy decisions. The programs used techniques such as role playing and game simulation, and they were often held at the regional level. Topics included the Clean Water Act, energy conservation, water-quality management, community municipal wastewater management, community flood-hazard management, forest service planning, and toxic substance control.

EPA's public involvement program in toxic substances (1979 to 1981) demonstrates the type and scale of EPA grant programs for training. In this million-dollar program, EPA funded both national and local environmental groups. National groups developed educational materials for community groups, including a handbook, a newsletter, a slide show, and a training guide. The guide covers both substantive material and methods of research and action. There was a national conference of local, environmental, labor, and civic leaders involved in toxic substance issues. In addition, EPA made 27 grants to local and state groups. Some of these grants went to universities and state or local League of Women Voters affiliates; others went to environmental groups. For instance, the Rutgers Journalism Resources Institute ran workshops on gathering, analyzing, and disseminating information, and Environmental Alternatives surveyed toxic substance problems in Louisville, Kentucky.

The toxic substance program was only one of several major public involvement programs that provided training resources to environmental groups. EPA's Waste Alert program funded half a dozen groups to hold regional conferences on waste issues. The American Public Health Association coordinated this effort, which also involved several major environmental membership groups and the League of Women Voters. While most EPA-funded training concentrated on specific issues, EPA also funded a handbook on citizen participation and several pamphlets on skills. These resources discuss working with the press, holding effective meetings, setting up advisory groups, and producing a newsletter.

EPA grants to environmental and other citizen groups were curtailed in 1981 with the change in administration. Related funds for public information were also reduced. The fiscal year (FY) 1981 estimate for all public participation activities was $7.5 million. The fiscal year 1982 estimate was $833,000, and these funds were primarily for public information activities.

Other training funds, previously earmarked for citizen action and environmental awareness and channeled through the Community Services Administration (established in 1975 to replace the Office of

Economic Opportunity) and the federal Office of Environmental Education, have also been reduced and/or reallocated under the Reagan administration.

There are no readily accessible records of how much community action money went for environmentally related programs, but a small percentage of the funds were used for this purpose. In reducing and redistributing the system of federal domestic assistance and categorical grants, the Omnibus Budget Reconciliation Act (1981) created several block grants. The Community Development Block Grant and Urban Development Action Grant not only reduced federal allocations, but the authority for these programs has shifted to states and localities. It is estimated that over 100,000 public service jobs, many of which were for support staff in community-based organizations, including environmental groups, were cut with the demise of the Comprehensive Employment and Training Act (CETA). Today, state agencies are providing training, especially in the areas of financial management and assistance to local governments. But the new emphasis of training efforts is on fostering local fiscal control, ensuring financial solvency to the locality, and promoting efficient resource allocation.

Between FY 1971 and 1977, $55 million was appropriated to the Office of Environmental Education in the federal Office of Education to fund environmental education. The monies were for grants and contracts with institutions of higher education, state, local, and regional agencies, research organizations, and other private and public agencies. The purpose of the grants was to educate the public in the problems of environmental quality and ecological balance. One grant provided initial funding for the New England Network, for example. From FY 1978 to 1982, no further appropriations for environmental education were made. However, the Elementary and Secondary Education Block Grant (1981) authorized state and local educational units use of funds to carry out selected activities from a full range of programs and projects—gifted and talented, ethnic heritage, arts, career education, environmental, health, legal, and citizenship education. The federal Office of Education is not monitoring how state units are spending these discretionary dollars. Therefore, it is difficult to know how much and where states are currently spending for environmental education.

Industry Support

Although corporations have not provided direct support for training the staff or members of environmental organizations, they have provided indirect support in a variety of ways.

For example, under the guidance of David Gray, an IBM vice-president of international organizations on loan to the New York office of the National Executive Service Corps,[49] IBM has developed a program of community executive training seminars. These programs ran weekly from January 1982 through September 1983 and trained 1,500 community leaders who were identified and brought into the program through endorsements of local IBM branch managers. The second phase of the project, now in progress, involves an informal agreement between General Electric, Xerox, and IBM to adapt corporate management training packages to the nonprofit setting. These training packages will be distributed to large volunteer organizations and may be of help to environmental organizations.

Corporations are major contributors to many educational institutions and are becoming an increasingly important source of general support for some environmental organizations. Some companies have provided large amounts of money for environmentally related research programs in universities, and these programs have not only increased scientific knowledge but also have provided training for students, a few of whom may go to work for environmental groups. Internships and regular employment with firms doing environmentally relevant work, such as chemical and forest-products companies, is an important form of training for many people.

Private Philanthropy

Only a fraction of 1 percent of private philanthropy in the United States goes to environment and conservation, and only a very small fraction of this is for training. However, private foundations have been a significant force in environmental training.

In the early 1970s a number of foundations spearheaded national efforts to fund training activities. These included the Charles Stewart Mott, Edna McConnell Clark, and Jessie Smith Noyes foundations. For example, the Mott Foundation funded the Institute of Man and Science, Rensselaerville, New York, an independent nonprofit center concerned with reviving the vitality and physical core of small towns and neighborhoods. The institute sponsored a series of leadership management workshops organized around the theme "Rebuild Your Organization and the Community." Other examples of training efforts funded primarily by foundations are cited throughout this report.

The Richard King Mellon Foundation is probably the leader in providing grants for environmental training. In addition to the internship and fellowship programs at Yale, discussed above, the foundation also funds an important training effort by the Appalachian Trail Club.

Foundations, including corporate foundations, appear to be increasing their funding of management assistance projects in the region or city in which they are located. For example, such projects have been funded by the New York Community Trust (New York City), the Medina Foundation (Puget Sound), and the Dayton Hudson Foundation (Minneapolis). Management assistance centers in Boston, New York, Philadelphia, Chicago, Minneapolis, Kansas City, Denver, Houston, Oklahoma City, Los Angeles, and San Francisco now rely on groups of foundations in their respective metropolitan areas.

References

1. Candace Ashmun, Comments on Training Needs Report, November 1983.

2. Interview conducted by Gail Bingham, April 1983.

3. Stuart Langton, *Learning Interests and Needs of Environmental Leaders in New England*, (Medford, Mass.: New England Environmental Network, Tufts University, 1978), p.3.

4. Letter to The Conservation Foundation, February 1983.

5. William L. Bryan, "Preventing Burnout in the Public Interest Community,"*Grantsmanship News*, March/April 1981, p.66.

6. Clem L. Zinger, Richard Dalsemer, and Helen Maguire, *Environmental Volunteers in America, Findings and Recommendations of the Steering Committee of the National Center for Voluntary Action's Environmental Program*. (Prepared for the U.S. Environmental Protection Agency), pp. 23, 24, 34.

7. Russell L. Brenneman, "A High Demand for Professionalism," Land Trust Exchange, Winter 1982-1983, p.16.

8. Bryan, "Preventing Burnout," p.66.

9. Association of New Jersey Environmental Commissions, Box 157, Mendham, NJ 07945.

10. Land Trust Exchange, Mount Desert, ME 04660.

11. New England Environmental Network, Lincoln Filene Center, Tufts University, Medford, MA 02155.

12. Northern Rockies Action Group, 9 Placer, Helena, MT 59601.

13. Sierra Club, 530 Bush Street, San Francisco, CA 94108.

14. League of Women Voters Education Fund, 1730 M Street, N.W., Washington, DC 20036.

15. This directory is available from Gale Research Co., Book Tower, Detroit, Michigan.

16. This journal is available from Lakewood Publications, Inc., Hennepin Ave., Minneapolis, MN 55403.

17. Available from the Edna McConnell Clark Foundation, 250 Park Ave., New York, NY 10017.

18. Nonprofit Management Association, c/o Alan Kumanoto, 611 W. 6th Street, Los Angeles, CA 90012.

19. The Foundation Center, 888 Seventh Ave., New York, NY 10019.

20. The Public Service Materials Center, 111 N. Central Ave., Hartsdale, NY 10530.

21. The Public Management Institute, 358 Brannan St., San Francisco, CA 94107.

22. Taft Corporation, 5125 MacArthur Blvd., N.W., Washington, DC 20016.

23. American Society for Training and Development, 600 Maryland Ave., S.W., Suite 305, Washington, DC 20025.

24. American Management Association, 135 W. 50th St., New York, NY 10020.

25. American Society of Association Executives, 1575 Eye Street, N.W., Washington, DC 20005.

26. National Training Laboratories, NTL Institute, P.O. Box 9155, Rosslyn Station, Arlington, VA 22209.

27. Anschutz Family Foundation, 2400 Anaconda Tower, 555 17th Street, Denver, CO 80202.

28. "Universities Add Spice to Executive Development,"*Training*, February 1983, p.77.

29. Volunteer: The National Center for Citizen Involvement, P.O. Box 4179, Boulder, CO 80306, and 1111 N. 19th Street, Suite 500, Arlington, VA 22209.

30. United Way of America, 801 N. Fairfax Street, Alexandria, VA 22314.

31. The Grantsmanship Center, 1031 S. Grand Ave., Los Angeles, CA 90015.

32. Karin Abarbanel, "The Grantsmanship Center: David vs. Goliath, Round Two,"*Foundation News*, March/April 1978, p.22.

33. Clarke Maylone, "The Field of Technical Assistance,"*Grantsmanship Center News*, March/April 1983, p.70.

34. Center for Community Change, 1000 Wisconsin Ave., N.W., Washington, DC 20007.

Community Technical Assistance Center, 307 Fourth Ave., Suite 1305, Pittsburgh, PA 15222.

Center for Management Assistance, One W. Armour Blvd., Kansas City, MO 64111.

Technical Assistance Center, 1385 So. Colorado Blvd., #504, Denver, CO 80222.

Community Training and Development, 1095 Market, Room 612, San Francisco, CA 94103.

35. The Support Center, 1309 L Street, N.W., Washington, DC 20005.

36. The Youth Project, 1555 Connecticut Ave., N.W., Washington, DC 20036.

37. Community Training and Development, 1095 Market, Room 612, San Francisco, CA 94103.

38. Addresses for these organizations can be provided by CTD or alternatively, from the organizations' national headquarters.

39. This report is available from the Charles Stewart Mott Foundation.

40. Citizen Involvement Training Project, 138 Hasbrouck, University of Massachusetts, Amherst, MA 01003.

41. Urban Environment Conference, 1314 14th Street, N.W., Washington, DC 20005.

42. Citizens Clearinghouse for Hazardous Waste, Box 926, Arlington, VA 22216.

43. According to data supplied in a 1980 report by the U.S. Department of Labor and U.S. Environmental Protection Agency, *Environmental Protection Careers Guidebook* (U.S. Dept. of Labor, Employment and Training Administration, 1980), there are over 1,200 specialized environmental programs offered in post-secondary schools. At the undergraduate and graduate levels, these programs are frequently located in a professional school of engineering or health sciences or in one of the resource sciences such as water, forestry, fisheries, etc.

There are 369 offerings in the general purpose environmental studies programs. These programs were developed in the 1970s when the environmental movement had great appeal. Rooted in inter- and multidisciplinary approaches, these programs stress the integration of different disciplines to achieve a holistic perspective and attempt to develop a student's problem-solving, as opposed to technical, capability. Excellent descriptions of 45 of these programs, mainly undergraduate, are found in Clay Schoenfield and John Disinger, eds., *Environmental Education in Action—II: Case Studies of Environmental Studies Programs in Colleges and Universities Today* (ERIC Clearinghouse for Science, Mathematics, and Environmental Education, Ohio State University, Columbus, Ohio, February 1978).

There is some general agreement that environmental studies program graduates with only a B.S. have had difficulty finding jobs, since entry-level positions are often defined in terms of an acknowledged discipline or technical skill.

44. Richard L. Perrine, "TSCA and the Universities: Educating the Environmental Chemical Professional,"*The Environmental Professional*, vol. 4, 1982, pp.187-200.

45. Center for Environmental Intern Programs, 629 Statler Office Bldg., Boston, MA 02116.

46. The German Marshall Fund of the United States, 11 Dupont Circle, Washington, DC 20036.

47. The CORO Foundation maintains three full-service centers in San Francisco, Los Angeles, and St. Louis. In addition, there is a recruiting center in New York and a summer internship program in Kansas City.

48. W.K. Kellogg Foundation, 400 North Avenue, Battle Creek, MI 49016.

49. National Executive Service Corps, 622 Third Avenue, 31st Floor, New York, NY 10017.

Chapter 4

Matching Needs, Resources, and Institutions

Training is an important need for most environmental groups, and most groups recognize the need for training. They do not, however, rank training as their highest priority when asked to compare this need with others. Understandably, there is a sharper focus on the immediate tasks and goals of the group. Training, although it may well be essential in fulfilling these tasks and goals, is a less-visible and thus lower-priority need.

Needs and Resources

Training needs and the ability to take advantage of training resources vary with the nature of the group and may vary for different types of people within the same group. For example, in the responses to The Conservation Foundation's questionnaire, "other membership recruiting techniques" received one of the highest overall ratings as a training need. But this need was primarily registered by smaller groups. Some of the larger groups have the opposite problem; they must deal with a heavy influx of new members and volunteers.

The training needs given highest priority in questionnaire responses were those related to fund-raising. This is not particularly surprising, given the chronic financial difficulties of most environmental groups. But this priority probably also reflects the need to adapt to changes in potential sources of funding, not just the need for money. For example, the ability to write the kinds of proposals that would appeal to government agencies is not as useful a skill as it used to be. Rather, groups need training in how to approach private foundations and corporations and in how to raise money through other techniques.

Another training need given a fair amount of priority by the groups studied is training in substantive policy issues. It should be noted, however, that, although the need for such training is important, improved understanding of public policy comes in broader forms than most other kinds of training. In a real sense, reading a good morning newspaper or one of the many environmental journals or newsletters is a form of training in policy issues. In fact, a survey by the New England Network found that written materials were the first choice of environmentalists among methods for learning about environmental policy.[1]

Some of the leaders of major national environmental groups interviewed for this report perceived their organizations as suffering from severe management difficulties. The reasons for these difficulties are probably diverse and thus will require diverse types of training. For example, some of the problems seem attributable to leaders or board members of the group, whereas other problems are traceable to flaws in accounting, personnel management, or other middle-management functions. Insofar as training can address these problems, the style and content of the training will have to be more or less individually tailored to a particular group and its particular management problems.

And sometimes training will not work. Lack of funds, particular personalities, or the management of a group by people with an exclusive focus on programmatic ends, among other factors, may prevent training from being used or render it ineffective if it is used.

The institutional resources available to meet the diverse training needs covered by our study are impressive. As indicated in the preceding chapter, there are a very large number of organizations, both profit and nonprofit, that either do or could provide training for environmental groups. The training organizations are located throughout the nation, and they provide an almost bewildering diversity of types of training available for various periods of time at different prices. It is difficult to name training needs for which the institutional resources to meet those needs do not exist, at least in major metropolitan areas. Thus, one clear conclusion of this study is that the creation of any new institutions to provide training is unnecessary and, if anything, probably would be counterproductive.

Despite the large number of training resources, very little of this training is directed specifically at the needs of environmental groups. The resources available to environmental groups to provide training related to policy areas have been severely reduced during the past several years. Little management training is now tailored specifically for environmental groups, although the general field of management training for nonprofit organizations is burgeoning. With some effort devoted to adaptation and linkage, these management training resources should be capable of serving the needs of the environmental community.

Linkage Between Needs and Resources

The greatest need that emerged from this study was to find ways to link the groups with training needs to the organizations that can fulfill those needs. Leaders of a number of major environmental groups expressed this need (see chapters 2 and 3), and replies to the questionnaire indicated that half the groups did not know a way to meet the training needs they identified. Dealing with this need involves two sets of related problems. First, many groups are not aware of the wealth of training resources available. They do not know that organizations exist which can give advice on staff-board relations or offer expert assistance in establishing an accounting system, for example. Second, even those groups aware of such resources do not know how to select the type of organization they need or which source of advice to choose.

The first of these problems may be rectified by establishing a clearinghouse for environmental training needs and resources. There might be a single national clearinghouse and/or regional clearinghouses. Several different types of services could be provided.

- The clearinghouse could maintain a directory of training resources available to environmental groups. The directory would be similar to *The Resource Directory for Funding and Managing Nonprofit Organizations*, published in 1982 and funded by the Edna McConnell Clark Foundation and the Exxon Foundation.[2] It would differ from this directory by aiming specifically at environmental groups, emphasizing management at least as much as funding, and being updated on a regular basis.
- The directory could be supplemented by individual advice, for a fee, on training resources.
- The clearinghouse could become an exchange, somewhat like the *Commerce Business Daily*, though obviously much smaller in scale. Environmental groups could list the type of training they seek, describing the tasks to be performed, the preferred qualifications and experience sought in a trainer, and procedures and deadlines for the submission of training proposals. Such a listing could then be sent routinely to trainers; trainers might be encouraged to subscribe. Such an exchange might improve

the ad hoc, word-of-mouth method, currently the most common way of locating consultants.

- The clearinghouse might publish a newsletter reporting on relevant foundation and corporate training grants; maintain a calendar of training courses and conferences; report on the use of new electronic capabilities and their adoption by enviromental organizations; analyze the effectiveness of various training methods; report on the experiences of the environmental groups in both providing and receiving training; prepare and distribute a bibliography of training materials; and provide information on new literature and developments related to training and management.

The clearinghouse, guided by a steering or advisory committee composed of members of environmental organizations and training experts, could be operated independently or as part of an existing organization.[4] It would require an initial start-up grant (probably in the $200,000 range), after which the clearinghouse might finance a portion of its expenses from fees and newsletter subscriptions.

Whether or not a clearinghouse is created, the development, publication, and dissemination of an annotated bibliography of core management materials would be very useful. The bibliography ought to cover the best books and manuals on nonprofit management topics and could be targeted either specifically to environmental groups or to a broader nonprofit audience.[5]

A clearinghouse will not solve all of the problems of linkage between environmental groups and training resources. Many smaller groups cannot subscribe to a newsletter and are unable to afford services provided by a clearinghouse, even if the rates were minimal. The problem of which training resource to select would remain for groups that had the funds to use such a resource. But the clearinghouse would fill an important gap and be a significant aid to environmental groups for taking advantage of the existing training resources.

Coordinating Environmental Trainers

Chapter 3 describes some training programs targeted specifically at environmental groups. Generally, the people involved in training environmental groups do not have extensive knowledge of one another, and there is no mechanism for comparing notes or coordinating efforts. As a start, a meeting of such trainers would help. The agenda for the meeting might include such topics as: How do the trainers' qualifications match the needs identified by environmental groups? What criteria should be used to evaluate training programs? How can those who most need training be reached? What are the alternatives for funding training programs? How might environmental trainers work with trainers in the general nonprofit field?

Policy Training

Training in substantive policy issues and in methods of policy analysis gives environmental groups the necessary information and understanding of issues to participate equally in policy debates with other parties, such as government and industry, which often have better access to information and expertise. It enables groups to take more informed positions on policy issues and to defend such positions more persuasively. As discussed in chapter 2, the groups perceive the need for such training and, as discussed in chapter 3, this is one area where existing training resources are meager. Current training in policy issues occurs either in the context of political mobilization, where the information is often one-sided, or in technical meetings, where policy implications may be ignored.

Providing policy training nationally is, on the whole, expensive, if for no other reason than because the geographical spread of environmental groups requires offering training courses (if that is the form the policy training takes) in a number of locations. However, short courses or briefing sessions given at a single location can be useful for groups in that geographical location and can be relatively inexpensive.

Groups such as the New England Network and Northern Lights in Montana currently are providing policy training on a regional basis. Such training is valuable and useful, but, given that a third of the groups responding to our survey said that most of the issues they dealt with were national in scope, there is also a need for national training programs. Also, on national issues, it is more efficient to develop a single basic training course (which can be modified for different states or regions) than to develop a number of different courses addressing the same issue.

It is unlikely that any source other than the federal government will have the money or inclination to fund continuing national policy training programs. Lacking federal funding for policy training, consideration should be given to private funding sources for pilot programs in policy training. The programs could be developed and delivered by universities or by environmental research organizations, although those who will receive the training should be involved in program development. The programs should be aimed at environmental groups yet open to a broader audience as well. They might use a variety of techniques, such as videotapes, simulation, and game playing, and issue briefs (such as those compiled by the Congressional Research Service). If a pilot program were successful (and the funding should include specific provisions for evaluation), it could be repeated in other locations, perhaps through state environmental coordinating groups or through the state land-grant colleges and universities.

Graduate-level Environmental Studies

As discussed in Chapter 3, graduate programs in environmental studies are at a crossroad. Their future direction, in some cases even their survival, is very much an open question. There is a need to examine the rationale for such programs, the problems they face in recruiting students and in placing graduates in jobs, and the way the programs should be funded. These questions may shed light not only on environmental studies but also on the more general question of how, if at all, colleges and universities should respond to important areas of public policy that do not fit into the normal academic disciplinary categories.

Apart from the basic questions related to environmental studies programs, more coordinated effort among the programs must occur. Although several existing associations, such as the National Association of Environmental Education[6] and the National Association of Environmental Professionals,[7] might provide this coordination, the academic deans do not participate in these associations. What is needed is some organization to take the initiative in calling the relevant people together and an organization to provide sponsorship for coordination efforts.

Coordination could take several forms. As a start, regular meetings to discuss common problems and explore solutions might be scheduled. Modest outside support might be necessary to help with travel expenses. These meetings might result in sharing of field station facilities, common efforts in job placement for students (including, perhaps, a unified listing of available positions), and joint efforts to improve the funding and prestige of environmental studies.

The role, condition, or problems of undergraduate environmental studies programs were not examined in this study. Although many of the problems of the graduate programs also are faced by undergraduate programs, some of the questions raised above are not applicable to undergraduate programs, and any consideration of undergraduate environmental studies programs requires a separate study.

Internships and Fellowships

Internships offer efficient training and could ameliorate several of the problems discussed above. Two kinds of internships deserve particular consideration—those that can improve the policy competence of the intern and environmental group and those that can upgrade the internal management of an environmental group.

Policy-oriented internships take several forms. The most common is for students, either graduate or undergraduate, to spend a few months working with an environmental group. This provides the students with a taste of the "real world" and may also benefit the group by bringing to it someone familiar with the current thinking and latest techniques developed in the academic world. Formal evaluations of these types of student internships have not (to our knowledge) been published, but, based at least on the experience of The Conservation Foundation, they have a very high payoff for both the student and the group in which he or she works.

A second form of policy internship is for academics to spend time working with an environmental group. This has been tried sporadically by a number of organizations. It is more difficult to make such arrangements succeed than to make student internships succeed, but the benefits could be even greater. Similarly, government officials or businessmen could spend a period of time working for an environmental group. The reverse arrangement, of having staff from an environmental group spend time in academia, government, or a business firm, has been tried occasionally and seems worthy of an expanded, regular attempt.

No internships orient toward improving the management of environmental groups. Perhaps exchanges among environmental groups or between business firms and such groups or schools of business or management and such groups would be an effective way of improving internal management. Retired businesspeople might be a pool of talent worth plumbing. The National Executive Service Corps (NESC), made up of retired business executives, places volunteers in organizations; its files list several thousand available volunteers.

There are NESC organizations in 13 cities and in 2 states. The services rendered by the retired executives range from reorganizing filing systems to planning and implementing strategies for fund-raising.

Management Training Program for Mid-size Groups

The questionnaire response showed a particularly high interest in management training for the staff of groups with between 10,000 and 100,000 members. Nearly 90 percent of these groups felt they needed training in fund-raising, use of volunteers, strategic planning, budgeting, personnel management, and use of office technology.

One way of addressing this need is to include environmental group managers in programs such as that offered by Community Training and Development (CTD), described in chapter 3 of this report. Components of the CTD program for professional development of non-profit managers include small problem-solving groups, access to corporate training programs as guests, and development of mentor relationships. A roundtable provides an opportunity for continued sharing of ideas and a forum for joint action.

Programs like CTD offer the kind of continued and in-depth learning not obtained in one-time workshops, the most common type of management training now available. The initiative in developing such programs where they do not now exist might be taken by management support organizations, universities, or environmental groups themselves. Although the environmental groups surveyed indicated a willingness to contribute to the costs, some scholarship assistance probably would be necessary.

Improving Management in the Larger Groups

In interviews, the larger environmental and conservation groups identified management as an important problem. Internships are one technique for improving management. Other techniques should be considered, however.

Larger groups can usually afford to pay for training. Perhaps a two- or three-day training course, covering subjects such as internal organization, board-staff relations, personnel management, and budgeting, would benefit such groups. Such training is available now, but if it were given by an environmental group, or designed with the advice and assistance of environmental groups, and were aimed specifically at the needs of other environmental groups, it might attract better attendance and have more effect.

One possibility is for a cluster of environmental groups to arrange joint training. Several groups, including the League of Women Voters, the American Association of University Women, and Business and Professional Women, have arranged joint training in personnel management for their staffs, for instance.

Insofar as the management problems of the larger groups are attributable to the leaders or board members of such groups, special training programs are necessary to attract and interest these high-level officials. Independent Sector,[8] an association of nonprofit organizations, in cooperation with Case Western Reserve University, has designed a management-improvement program aimed at top executives that should be applicable to the leadership of environmental organizations.

Conclusion

The great diversity of environmental groups, of training needs, and of methods and organizations to meet these needs makes it difficult to generalize about the appropriateness of training for environmental groups. However, it is clear from this survey that the environmental community needs both management and policy training.

The need for training is generally given lower priority by environmental groups than are other needs more obviously related to the programmatic goals of the organizations. Environmental groups are often short of funds, and programmatic goals take priority over more instrumental needs such as training. But training can improve the fund-raising skills of groups as well as increase the effectiveness and efficiency with which the funds are used.

Most of the existing management training resources have not been aimed at or used by environmental groups. Creating linkages is probably the most important step in fulfilling management training needs. Improving the policy skills and knowledge of environmental groups takes precedence: here, additional funding for policy training probably constitutes the greatest need.

Meeting training needs will require money. Given the resource constraints of environmental groups and the priority that they give to programmatic goals, it is unlikely that they will devote a significant part of their existing funds to training. Thus, if the management and policy skills of environmental groups are to be upgraded, new support from foundations, corporations, and the government is necessary. The Conservation Foundation hopes that this report will stimulate both funding sources and environmental groups to become more aware of the types of training needs that exist.

References

1. Stuart Langton, *Learning Interests and Needs of Environmental Leaders in New England*. (Medford, Mass.: New England Environmental Network, Tufts University, 1978), p.3.

2. Edna McConnell Clark Foundation, 250 Park Avenue, New York, NY 10017.

3. M. Argosh and M. Troutman, "Cutting in on the Bull and Bear: Business School Can Teach You the Steps," *Community Jobs*, November 1981, p.3.

4. The Environmental Task Force, 1346 Connecticut Ave., N.W., Washington, DC 20036, has initiated some efforts to coordinate and share experiences among environmental groups. However, these have been colored by the more activist efforts of the Task Force.

5. A start toward such a bibliography was made by Clarke Maylone in his unpublished report "A Community Action Agency Core Library: The Best Books and Manuals on Management and Mission Subjects for Community Action Leaders," commissioned by the Community Services Administration in 1981.

6. National Association of Environmental Education, P.O. Box 400, Troy, OH 45373.

7. National Association of Environmental Professionals, P.O. Box 9400, Washington, DC 20016.

8. Independent Sector, 1828 L Street, N.W., Washington, DC 20036.

Appendix A

Methodology and Sample

To ascertain what training was needed by environmental groups, what training was being provided, what obstacles existed to obtaining training, and what new initiatives, if any, were desirable, staff members of The Conservation Foundation reviewed the existing literature, sent a questionnaire to environmental groups, and interviewed leaders of environmental groups, providers of training, and funding sources. (The questionnaire is reproduced as appendix B.) In addition, a small conference of graduate-level environmental educators and representatives of foundations that had funded environmental training efforts was held in June 1983.

Training needs can be assessed both by environmental groups themselves and by training specialists. Although a number of training specialists were consulted, this report is based largely on perceptions of environmental groups. Their perceptions are as important as any attempt to evaluate their needs objectively. The resources (both time and money) of the groups also will influence the extent to which they can take advantage of any training offered. Therefore, both the perceptions of and resources of the groups studied were evaluated.

Methodology

About 400 professional associations; communication, education, and research organizations; and activist groups were selected to receive the questionnaire; 225 questionnaires were completed and returned. About a quarter of the groups are national in scope. The remaining three-fourths are state and local organizations chosen to cover the spectrum of groups as well as to provide mixed geographical representation.

Selection of the questionnaire recipients was complicated by the absence of a single, comprehensive list or directory of environmental organizations from which to obtain a representative sample. Thus, the list of recipients had to be put together by using several different sources.

The 1983 *Conservation Directory* was used as the basic source for national groups. Every third nongovernmental national U.S. group listed in the directory was selected, with the following modifications: (1) all members of the Natural Resources Council of America (44 groups) were included, because council members constitute the major national environmental groups; (2) several other national groups, such as the Environmental Law Institute and the Environmental Task Force, were deemed particularly important for the survey, although they were not members of the council, and were added; (3) about 20 groups were deleted from the list derived from the directory because they were not within this study's scope. These included university and business programs as well as some private organizations, such as the National Geographic Society.

State and local organizations were determined by four different steps. First, 35 organizations, most of which serve as coordinating groups for their states, were chosen. Second, three geographical regions were selected for special emphasis to get more extensive representation of local groups. About 50 groups were randomly selected from each of three directories, chosen for being recent and covering the eastern, midwestern, and far-western sections of the United States. To make the lists more consistent, most university-affiliated and quasi-governmental groups, as well as nature preserves and a few groups peripherally related to the environment, were omitted. The directories used were: *Directory of Environmental Groups in New England*, U.S. Environmental Protection Agency, Region I, January 1981; *Environmental Hotline*, U.S. Environmental Protection Agency, Region V, 1981; *California Environmental Directory: A Guide to Organization and Resources*, 3rd Edition, California Institute of Public Affairs, Claremont Colleges, 1981.

Third, about 100 state groups were randomly selected from the *Conservation Directory*'s list of state citizen groups. Groups from states covered by the regions chosen for special concentration and listed above were omitted. Fourth, 17 Sierra Club chapters were randomly selected from the club's overall list, because these chapters were not included in the *Conservation Directory*.

The final composition of the groups surveyed is shown in table A.1. Every effort was made to ensure a high rate of response. The questionnaire was mailed with a personally addressed and signed letter and a stamped return envelope. A follow-up postcard was mailed to all recipients two weeks later. Four weeks after the original mailing, a second copy of the questionnaire with an appropriate letter was mailed to those groups that had not yet responded. Finally, major national groups that had not responded were telephoned with a request to fill out and return the questionnaire.

In all, 225 completed questionnaires were returned. We consider the completed questionnaires, on the whole, to be a reasonably representative sample of environmental organizations, but the level and representativeness of the response were affected by several factors. Although environmental and conservation groups were defined in the cover letter as including research groups and professional societies as well as activist groups, about a dozen professional societies replied that they did not consider themselves environmental groups or did not find the questionnaire applicable to their work. Thus, this type of organization is probably underrepresented. The questionnaire did not describe The Conservation Foundation. A few letters indicated concern that the foundation might be an industrial front or a right-wing organization; a few others viewed the questionnaire as a market survey, indicating an intention by The Conservation Foundation to compete with existing training programs.

The content of the responses, particularly the responses related to policy, was influenced by the Environmental Protection Agency (EPA) controversy, which reached its height just after the questionnaires were distributed. Any issue other than improving EPA's performance was irrelevant to some groups. All answers also depended very much on who filled out the questionnaire; different people from the same organization do, of course, see training needs differently.

Respondents found it difficult to distinguish between training needs for members and staff. Just over half the questionnaires included ratings for group members. Members also were equated with volunteers by some groups, although in some cases volunteers might be properly classified as staff.

To supplement the questionnaire responses, a number of interviews were conducted. William K. Reilly, president of The Conservation Foundation, interviewed the heads of 14 major national environmental organizations. Gail Bingham interviewed providers and users of training in Washington State and California. Project staff had numerous telephone and in-person interviews with other representatives of environmental groups and with providers of training for both environmental and other groups. Frequently, interviews uncovered a view of an organization that differed from the questionnaire response.

Not surprising was that the research revealed a variety of training needs and, perhaps more surprising, a large number and variety of resources to meet these needs.

Characteristics of Questionnaire Sample

The questionnaire results provide a profile of about 225 environmental groups by location, age, membership, staff, function, issues, geographical scope, and size and source of annual budgets. (See figure A.1 and table A.2.) As mentioned above, the groups in this sample are believed reasonably to represent the diversity of all environmental and conservation groups.

Location

As the map (figure A.1) shows, the groups in our sample operate in all parts of the country. There is a heavy concentration of national groups in Washington, D.C. Slightly over a fourth of the responding groups are located in the Northeast, whereas the West, South, and North Central regions each has about a fifth.

Age

Some groups that are now viewed as part of the environmental movement were actually founded as much as a hundred years before Earth Day in 1970. These older groups dominate in size. However, nearly two-thirds of the groups responding to the questionnaire were created after 1960.

Membership

Four-fifths of the groups have dues-paying members. About a quarter of the groups are affiliates of other organizations. Nearly half of the groups have under 1,000 members; 6 percent have over 100,000.

Staff

Staffing patterns are a major variable among environmental groups. Just over half the groups surveyed have at least one full-time paid staff person. Three-fifths have a full-time administrative head, some of them volunteer. About 10 percent of the groups have full-time volunteers. Most staffs are small. Only 15 percent of the groups surveyed have more than 10 full-time paid staff members.

Functions

Education and communication were reported as functions by all the groups who filled out the questionnaire. Litigation is the least common function. While 15 percent identified litigation as of crucial importance, 58 percent said it is not a function of their organizations. More common functions are community organizing, lobbying, policy development, and research. Two-thirds of the groups engage in these activities to some extent.

Issues

Nearly half the groups address land-use issues, whereas over a third deal with air and water pollution control. Energy, forestry, toxic substances, hazardous waste, other waste management, and wildlife are each addressed by between 15 percent and 20 percent of the groups. Work on other issues, such as health and urban issues and historic preservation, is done by 42 percent of the groups. Among all groups, 30 percent identified themselves as single-issue groups.

Geographical Scope

Most groups address issues on more than one geographical level. The state is the most common arena for action, followed by the local community. Almost all of the groups do some work at the regional, state, and local levels. A third of the groups said most of their issues are national; another half of the groups work at the national level at least some of the time. Although the survey did not include international groups, half of those responding said they work on the international level some of the time.

Source and Size of Budgets

About a third of the groups have annual budgets under $10,000. Only 3 percent of the groups in the survey, which included almost all major environmental groups, have annual budgets of over $600,000.

Membership dues are of crucial importance to nearly half the groups as a source of funds. Direct mail is used by two-thirds of the groups, although it accounts for over half the income for only 10 percent of the groups. Large donations are also important to many groups. Government grants are more than a fourth of the budgets for only a tenth of the groups.

Table A.1

Source of Groups Selected to Receive Questionnaire

Source	Number of Groups
National groups from *Conservation Directory*	83
Natural Resources Council of America members	44
State groups from *Conservation Directory*	117
State coordinating groups	35
State and local groups from regional directories	115
Sierra Club chapters	17
Total number selected	411

Figure A.1
Geographic Distribution of Survey Respondents

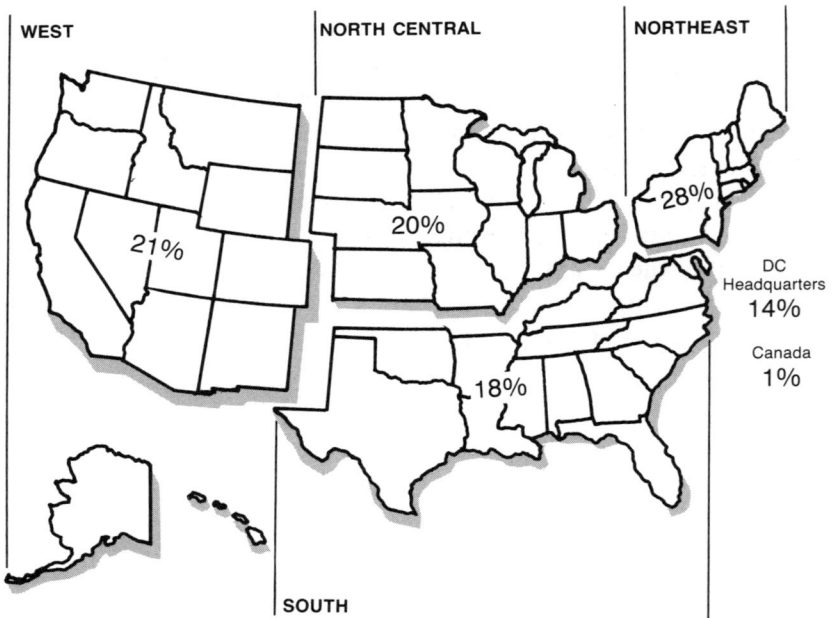

Figures add to more than 100% because of rounding.

Source: U.S. Bureau of the Census.

Table A.2

**Characteristics of Environmental Groups Sampled
by Percentage of Groups**

Age

Year Founded	1870-1919	1920-1959	1960-1969	1970-1982
	11	23	28	36

Size of Membership

Number of Members	0	1-100	101-1000	1001-10,000	10,000-100,000	100,000 +
	19	6	32	30	10	5

Staff

	0	1	2-5	6-10	11-20	21-99	100 +
Full-time paid	45	12	18	10	8	4	3
Part-time paid	65	15	15	2	2	–	–
Full-time volunteer	88	6	3	1	1	–	–
Part-time volunteer	56	7	14	8	16	–	–

Importance of Functions

	Important	Occasional	Not a Function
Community organizing	24	45	31
Education and communication	90	10	–
Litigation	15	28	58
Lobbying	33	39	28
Policy development	45	39	16
Research	38	43	19

Issues Addressed

Air/Water pollution control	38
Energy	18
Forestry	18
Land use	49
Toxics/hazardous waste	20
Waste management	15
Wildlife	19
Other	42

Table A.2 continued

Geographical Scope of Work

	Most Issues Are*	Some Issues Are*	Not Concerned with Such Issues
International	7	47	47
National	34	53	13
Regional	20	69	11
State	54	43	2
Local	45	47	8

*These add up to more than 100 percent because some issues may be addressed on more than one level.

Size of Annual Budget

$100-1,000	1,001-10,000	10,001-50,000	50,001-100,000	100,001-600,000	600,000-+
8	26	15	8	38	3

Source of Funds

	50% or More	25-50%	5-25%	Below 5%	Not a Source
Direct mail	12	18	25	11	34
Endowment	2	4	16	18	61
Government grants and contracts	4	6	12	17	61
Individual large donors	15	22	19	22	23
Dues	48	23	13	3	14
Publications	6	10	14	34	36
Other	16	27	18	11	28

Appendix B
The Questionnaire

TRAINING QUESTIONNAIRE

Instructions: Where numbers are given next to answer categories, please *circle* the number by your answer.

1. Name of Organization _____

2. Address _____
   _____

3. Telephone Number _____

4. Name of person responding to questionnaire
   _____

5. Position of person responding _____

6. Would you like us to send you a complimentary summary of the study results? (circle one number)
   1. Yes   2. No

A. Questions about your organization

7. What year was your organization started? _____

8. Does your organization have dues-paying members?
   1. Yes   2. No   3. Other (please specify)
   _____

9. If the answer to question 8 is yes, how many members do you have? _____

9.1 Of these members, how many are organizations rather than individuals? _____

10. Is your organization a local affiliate of a regional or national organization?
    1. Yes   2. No

11. If the answer to question 10 was yes, what organizations are you affiliated with? _____

12. How many individual staff members does your organization have? (Please put number of staff members in each column.)

	Full-Time Paid	Part-Time Paid	Full-Time Volunteer	Part-Time Volunteer
Non-clerical personnel	____	____	____	____
Clerical and other support personnel	____	____	____	____

13. Does your organization have a full-time administrative head (i.e., President, Executive Director, etc.)?
    1. Yes   2. No   3. Other (please specify)
    _____

14. How would you describe the functions your organization serves? (circle one number for each function)

	Important Function	Occasional Function	Not a Function
Community organizing	1	2	3
Education & Communication	1	2	3
Litigation	1	2	3
Lobbying	1	2	3
Policy Development	1	2	3
Research	1	2	3
Other (please describe) _____			

15. Which issue or issues is your organization primarily concerned with (i.e., air pollution, forest management, etc.)?

_____

_____

16. What is the particular geographical scope of the issues your organization works on? Please note that while air pollution, for example, has international dimensions, if you only deal with local air pollution issues you should treat it as a local issue for the purposes of this question. (please circle one number on each line)

	Most Issues Are	Some Issues Are	Not Concerned With With Such Issues
International	1	2	3
National	1	2	3
Regional (multi-state)	1	2	3
State	1	2	3
Local	1	2	3

17. What is the current annual budget of your organization?
$ _____

18. What is the importance of each of the following sources of funds for your organization's budget this year? (please circle one number on each line)

	Crucial (50% or more)	Very Important (25-50%)	Somewhat Important (5-25%)	Minor Source (below 5%)	Not a Source
Direct mail appeals	1	2	3	4	5
Endowment	1	2	3	4	5
Government grants & contracts	1	2	3	4	5
Individual large donors	1	2	3	4	5

Membership dues	1	2	3	4	5
Publications	1	2	3	4	5
Other (please specify)	1	2	3	4	5

B. Questions about the need for training

Listed below are a number of subjects for which training could potentially be provided to groups like yours. We would like you to assess the extent to which further training in each of these areas is needed by *your* staff (S) and membership (M) (if applicable) by circling the S and M in the appropriate columns. For example, for question 19.1 if training in fund raising is a high-priority training need for both the staff and members of your organization you should circle both the "M" and the "S" in the first column. If fund raising is a high-priority training need for the staff and unimportant for membership you should circle the "S" in the first column and "M" in the third. If you circle an "M" and/or an "S" in the fourth column, "not needed because already provided," it will be very helpful to us if you would indicate on the questionnaire how and by whom the training was provided.

For my organization at the present time, training in *(skill area)* is:

Skill area:	A high-priority need		Somewhat needed		Not needed because skill is not important		Not needed because training already provided	
19.1 Fund-raising through direct mail	M	S	M	S	M	S	M	S
19.2 Obtaining government and foundation grants	M	S	M	S	M	S	M	S
19.3 Other methods for raising funds	M	S	M	S	M	S	M	S
19.4 Accounting and financial management	M	S	M	S	M	S	M	S
19.5 Budgeting	M	S	M	S	M	S	M	S
19.6 Personnel management, including hiring, staffing patterns, and staff benefits	M	S	M	S	M	S	M	S
19.7 Office management, including supervisory skills	M	S	M	S	M	S	M	S

19.8 Use of office technology, i.e., word processing, etc.	M	S	M	S	M	S	M	S
19.9 Use of volunteers, interns	M	S	M	S	M	S	M	S

Reminder: Your responses to the items in question 19 should be based on your organization's *current training* needs, not on the general importance of the subjects.

19.10 Long-range planning, strategic planning	M	S	M	S	M	S	M	S
19.11 Specialized skills development (e.g., real estate management, financial investment strategies)	M	S	M	S	M	S	M	S
19.12 Use of mediation and negotiation for environmental disputes	M	S	M	S	M	S	M	S
19.13 Board-staff relations	M	S	M	S	M	S	M	S
19.14 How to research an issue	M	S	M	S	M	S	M	S
19.15 Library services and information retrieval	M	S	M	S	M	S	M	S
19.16 Background briefings on policy issues	M	S	M	S	M	S	M	S
19.17 Economics of environmental policies	M	S	M	S	M	S	M	S
19.18 Particular policy issues (please specify)	M	S	M	S	M	S	M	S
19.19 Press relations	M	S	M	S	M	S	M	S
19.20 Lobbying	M	S	M	S	M	S	M	S
19.21 Participation in electoral campaigns	M	S	M	S	M	S	M	S
19.22 Direct mail to recruit new members; membership lists	M	S	M	S	M	S	M	S
19.23 Other techniques for membership recruiting	M	S	M	S	M	S	M	S
19.24 Editing, production and marketing of books and pamphlets	M	S	M	S	M	S	M	S

19.25 Editing and production
      of newsletters   M S   M S   M S   M S

19.26 Conference planning
      and management   M S   M S   M S   M S

19.27 Networking with other
      groups, coalition
      building   M S   M S   M S   M S

19.28 Local group
      organizing   M S   M S   M S   M S

19.29 Litigation   M S   M S   M S   M S

19.30 Relating to the
      federal government   M S   M S   M S   M S

19.31 Relating to state or
      local government   M S   M S   M S   M S

19.32 Other (please describe)

_____

_____

_____

_____

_____

20. Please list below the numbers (i.e., 19.4, 19.7, etc.) of the two or
    three of the above that are the most important training needs of
    your organization and explain briefly why they are important to your
    organization at this time.

_____

_____

_____

_____

21. Are you aware of existing programs or institutions which could
    meet any of your organization's high-priority training needs?
                    1. Yes   2. No

22. If you answered yes to question 21, would you please identify as
    completely as possible the programs or institutions which could
    meet (or have met) some or all of your organization's training
    needs.

_____

_____

_____

23. Overall, how would you rate the training needs of your organization
    compared with its other needs?

        1. One of our most important needs
        2. Important, but not as important as some of our other needs

3. Not very important
4. Of little importance

24. What are the obstacles, if any, to your organization providing additional training for its staff or members?

_____

_____

_____

25. Does your organization provide formal training of any kind (such as providing courses, orientation sessions, etc.) for its staff, members, or others? If so, would you please briefly describe the training provided.

_____

_____

_____

_____

26. Does your organization currently have a budget for training activities?

        1. Yes   2. No

27. If the answer to question 26 was yes, how much money is currently budgeted for training? $ _____

28. If a top-quality two-day conference or workshop were given on one or more training skill areas which are a high priority for your organization, what is the most that you think your organization would be willing to pay (for fees, transportation, lodging, and other expenses) for a staff person or member to attend?

1. Nothing	5. $201-300	9. $601-800
2. $1-50	6. $301-400	10. $801-1,000
3. $51-100	7. $401-500	11. More than $1,000
4. $101-200	8. $501-600	12. Don't know

29. If the above conference or workshop lasted for one week, how much do you think your organization would be willing to pay?

1. Nothing	5. $201-300	9. $601-800
2. $1-50	6. $301-400	10. $801-1,000
3. $51-100	7. $401-500	11. More than $1,000
4. $101-200	8. $501-600	12. Don't know

30. If a one-semester course in a nearby college or university were offered on a subject which was a high priority for your organization, what is the most that you think your organization would be willing to pay for a staff person or member to take the course?

1. Nothing	5. $201-300	9. $601-800
2. $1-50	6. $301-400	10. $801-1,000
3. $51-100	7. $401-500	11. More than $1,000
4. $101-200	8. $501-600	12. Don't know

31. In the next year, how much time during the year do you think the person in your organization who could most benefit from training would be willing and able to spend receiving such training?
    1. More than 2 weeks
    2. 1-2 weeks
    3. 3-6 days
    4. 1-2 days
    5. Would not have any time
    6. Don't know

32. If an experienced consultant, or an expert from another environmental organization, could be made available to your organization to provide advice on a subject which was a high priority for your organization, how much do you think your organization would be willing to pay per day to obtain such advice?
    1. Nothing
    2. $1-50
    3. $51-100
    4. $101-200
    5. $201-300
    6. $301-400
    7. $401-500
    8. $501-600
    9. $601-800
    10. $801-1,000
    11. More than $1,000
    12. Don't know

33. What if an environmental or conservation organization offered internships where someone from your organization could work in that organization for a brief period of time to acquire skills needed by your organization? How useful to your organization do you think such an arrangement would be?
    1. Extremely useful
    2. Very useful
    3. Somewhat useful
    4. Not very useful
    5. Not useful at all
    6. Don't know

34. How does your organization find out about training opportunities? (circle more than one if appropriate)
    1. Colleagues
    2. Newsletters
    3. Promotional material
    4. Does not find out
    5. Other (please specify) _____
    _____

35. How easy or difficult has it been for your organization to find out about training opportunities appropriate to its needs?
    1. Very ease
    2. Somewhat easy
    3. Somewhat difficult

    4. Very difficult
    5. Don't know

36. Some people have suggested that there is a need for a new institution to provide training for environmental and conservation groups,
while others maintain that training needs are being adequately met
now. If a new institution were proposed whose purpose would be to
conduct training for environmental organizations what position or
attitude do you think your organization would be likely to take
toward the proposal?
    1. Strongly favor
    2. Somewhat favor
    3. Neutral
    4. Oppose
    5. Strongly oppose
    6. Don't know

C. Questions about environmental policy

37. Please briefly describe the environmental policy issues that you
consider the most important facing the U.S. today.

_____
_____
_____

38. Do you think that new policy ideas need to be developed to address the environmental problems faced by the U.S. and the world
or do you think we already know what needs to be done? New
ideas are:
    1. Badly needed
    2. Somewhat needed
    3. Not needed
    4. Don't know

39. If you responded to the above question that new ideas were
somewhat or badly needed, please briefly list the policy areas
where new ideas are needed.

_____
_____
_____

40. If a new institution were proposed to do research on environmental
policy and to develop new policy ideas and approaches what position or attitude do you think your organization would be likely to
take toward the proposal?
    1. Strongly favor
    2. Somewhat favor
    3. Neutral
    4. Oppose

5. Strongly oppose
6. Don't know

41. Please give us any other comments you think would be helpful regarding unmet needs of environmental organizations.

_____
_____
_____
_____

Thank you very much for your cooperation.

Appendix C

Training Needs by
Individual Skill

Fund-Raising and Membership Recruitment
Needs by Percentage of Groups

Number Responding			High Priority	Somewhat Needed	Not Important	Skill Provided
	19.1	*Fund-raising through direct mail*				
112		members	20	21	50	9
175		staff	33	29	19	19
	19.2	*Obtaining government and foundation grants*				
108		members	17	25	53	6
171		staff	32	35	19	13
	19.3	*Other methods for raising funds*				
111		members	35	29	30	6
174		staff	46	34	10	9
	19.22	*Direct mail to recruit new members*				
107		members	19	28	42	13
175		staff	37	30	17	16
	19.23	*Other membership-recruiting techniques*				
106		members	31	30	31	8
173		staff	49	30	14	8

**Internal Management
Needs by Percentage of Groups**

Number Responding		High Priority	Somewhat Needed	Not Important	Skill Provided
	19.4 *Accounting and financial management*				
98	members	5	26	49	20
166	staff	13	43	15	30
	19.5 *Budgeting*				
103	members	6	29	49	17
163	staff	14	43	16	27
	19.6 *Personnel management*				
103	members	5	13	72	12
163	staff	12	32	35	22
	19.7 *Office management*				
101	members	5	13	71	11
161	staff	12	40	29	19
	19.8 *Use of office technology*				
97	members	10	11	68	10
170	staff	25	33	26	16
	19.9 *Use of volunteers*				
107	members	35	32	24	9
172	staff	33	45	10	12
	19.10 *Strategic planning*				
109	members	26	35	35	5
167	staff	32	47	12	10
	19.11 *Specialized skills*				
103	members	2	23	69	6
162	staff	8	29	51	12
	19.13 *Board-staff relations*				
104	members	11	21	58	11
164	staff	12	38	32	18

Research and Policy Training
Needs by Percentage of Groups

Number Responding		High Priority	Somewhat Needed	Not Important	Skill Provided
	19.14 *How to research and issue*				
104	members	13	38	33	16
167	staff	16	41	16	28
	19.15 *Library services and information retrieval*				
105	members	8	29	43	22
165	staff	12	35	23	31
	19.16 *Background briefing on policy issues*				
104	members	14	36	36	14
165	staff	15	41	27	18
	19.17 *Economics of environmental policies*				
104	members	22	38	30	10
168	staff	21	42	24	13
	19.18 *Particular policy issues*				
66	members	20	23	44	15
96	staff	22	20	39	21

Training Needs in Communication Skills
Needs by Percentage of Groups

Number Responding		High Priority	Somewhat Needed	Not Important	Skill Provided
	19.12 *Use of mediation and negotiation*				
111	members	13	34	46	7
164	staff	9	36	46	9
	19.19 *Press relations*				
115	members	17	40	30	13
171	staff	24	46	11	19
	19.20 *Lobbying*				
112	members	16	37	35	13
169	staff	14	34	29	24
	19.21 *Participation in electoral campaigns*				
116	members	11	20	63	6
156	staff	7	7	68	9
	19.24 *Editing, production, and marketing of books and pamphlets*				
100	members	5	27	58	10
169	staff	23	32	27	18
	19.25 *Editing and production of newsletters*				
100	members	16	29	36	19
171	staff	25	38	9	28
	19.26 *Conference planning and management*				
107	members	7	35	46	13
168	staff	12	47	21	20
	19.27 *Networking and coalition building*				
112	members	17	33	36	14
171	staff	15	44	19	22
	19.28 *Local group organizing*				
114	members	25	27	34	14
163	staff	19	36	30	15
	19.29 *Litigation*				
103	members	4	17	67	13
166	staff	6	21	55	18
	19.30 *Relating to federal government*				
112	members	9	39	38	14
169	staff	11	40	28	21
	19.31 *Relating to state or local government*				
114	members	25	35	22	17
169	staff	23	36	10	23

Index

ACCORD Associates, 19
American Association of University Women, 89
American Management Association, 58, 60
American Public Health Association, 75
American Society of Association Executives, 58, 60
American Society for Training and Development, 1, 57-58, 62
Anderson, Nancy W., 51
Anschutz Family Foundation, 59
Appalachian Trail Club, 78
Association Management, 58
Association of New Jersey Environmental Commissions, 49, 55

Better Air Coalition, 74
BNA Communications, Inc., 57
Brenneman, Russell L., 47
Bryan, William L., 46-47
Budget. *See* Funding sources
Business and Professional Women, 89

California, University of. *See* UCLA
Case Western Reserve University, 89
Center for Community Change, 62
Center for Environmental Intern Programs, 70
Center for Management Assistance, 62

Chemical Substances Information Network, 49
Citizen Involvement Training Project, 65
Citizens Clearinghouse for Hazardous Wastes, 65-66
Claremont Graduate School, 72
Colorado Mountain Club, 48
Columbia University, 59
Commerce Business Daily, 83
Communications, 17-22
    comparative need for, *9*
    need for, by environmental groups, *18, 20, 21*
Community Development Block Grant, 76
Community Jobs, 65
Community-organizing training centers, 64-66
Community Services Administration, 75-76
Community Technical Assistance Center, 62
Community Training and Development (program), 62-63, 88
Comprehensive Employment and Training Act, 45, 76
Coro Foundation, 72

Dayton Hudson Foundation, 78
Department of Education, U.S., 50, 74, 76
Duke University, 41, 68
Dyer, Polly, 45

Earth Day, 10, 47

Edna McConnell Clark Foundation, 57, 77, 83
Education, 17-22
  and burnout prevention, 46-48
  comparative importance of, *9*
  need for, by environmental groups, *18, 20, 21*
Elementary and Secondary Education Block Grant, 76
Environmental Action Foundation, 56
Environmental Alternatives, 75
Environmental groups
  attitudes of, toward new training institutions, 37-38, *38*
  and burnout prevention, 46-48
  diversity of, 1-3
  interviews with leaders of, 38-42
  ranking of training needs by, *27, 28, 29, 30, 31, 32, 34-35*
  training needs of, 7-38
  training provided by, 33-36, 42, 48-56, *30, 32*
  use of environmental studies programs by, 73
  willingness of, to pay for training, 36-37, *37*
  see also Resources
Environmental Literature, 73
Environmental Protection Agency, U.S., 49, 74-75
Environmental Studies Center, 73
Environmental studies programs
  as a discipline, 67-68
  Duke University, 68
  profiles of selected, 68-70
  as training resource, 86-87
  UCLA, 68-69
  University of Michigan, 69-70
Exxon Foundation, 57, 83

Fell, George B., 46
Fellowships. *See* Internships

Fluharty, Marty, 52
Fortune 500 companies, 59
Foundation Center, The, 57
Funding sources, 74-78
  effect of federal policy on, 3-5, 76
  governmental, 74-76
  industry, 76-77
  private philanthropic, 77-78
Fund-raising
  comparative importance of, *9*
  need for, by environmental groups, *9, 10, 11*

General Electric, 77
Georgetown University, 59
German Marshall Fund, 72
Gibbs, Lois, 66
Government. *See* Funding sources, governmental
Grantsmanship Center, The, 60-61
Grantsmanship Center News, 60, 61
Gray, David, 77
Group size. *See* Training needs, ranking of

Harbinger Communications, 63-64
Harvard University, 41, 59
Heywood, Ann M., 57
Highlander Center, 64-65
"Human Resource Development" (catalogue), 57

IBM, 77
Independent Sector, 89
Industry. *See* Funding sources, industry
Institute for Applied Behavioral Science, 59

Institute for Environmental
Studies, 45
Institute for European
Environmental Policy, 72
Institute of Man and Science, 77
Institutions
attitudes toward new, for training, 37-38, 41, *38*
American Management Association, 58, 60
American Society of Association Executives, 58, 60
American Society for Training
and Development, 1, 57-58,
62
clearinghouse, 83-84
community-organizing training
centers, 64-66
The Grantsmanship Center,
60-61
management support organizations, 61-64
National Training Laboratories,
59
publications, 57, *18, 20, 21*
traditional, providing training,
56-60
United Way, 60, 63
universities, 59-60, 66-73, 86-87
Volunteer: National Center for
Citizen Involvement, 60
Internships
and PIRGs, 72-73
as training resources, 86-87
UCLA, 70
Yale University, 70-72
Issues. *See* Policy development

Jessie Smith Noyes Foundation,
77

Kellogg Foundation, W. K., 65, 72
Kennard, Byron, 1

Land Trust Exchange, 49-50, 55
League of Women Voters, 4,
53-55, 75, 89
Leduc, Robert F., 59
Lincoln Filene Center for Citizen-
ship and Public Affairs, 50,
51
Lincoln Institute of Land Policy,
49
Litigation. *See* Communications
Lobbying. *See* Communications
Love Canal, 66, 73

McDonald Foundation, 64
Maine Audubon Society, 48
Management, internal, 12-17
comparative need for, *9*
need for, by environmental
groups, 40, *13, 15, 16*
training resources for, 88-89
Management Assistance Group, 62
Management Center, The 63
Management support organiza-
tions, 61-64
Community Training and
Development (program),
62-63
Support Center, The, 62
Youth Project, The, 62
Maryland, University of, 60
Massachusetts Institute of
Technology, 59
Massachusetts, University of, 65
Maylone, Clark, 61
Mediation. *See* Communications
Mediation Institute, 19
Medina Johnson Foundaton, 64,
78
Mellon Foundation, Andrew W.,
68
Mellon Foundation, Richard King,
70, 77-78
Membership recruitment, 8-12

comparative need for, *9*
need for, by environmental
    groups, *9, 10, 11*
Michigan, University of, 69-70
Mott Foundation, Charles
    Stewart, 64, 77

National Association of
    Environmental Education, 86
National Association of
    Environmental Professionals,
    66, 86
National Executive Service Corps,
    63, 77, 87-88
National Training Laboratories, 59
Natural Areas Association, 46
Negotiation. *See* Communications
New England Environmental Net-
    work, 46, 50-51, 55, 76, 82,
    85
New Jersey Environmental
    Congress, 49
New York Community Trust, 78
New York, State University of, at
    Buffalo, 73
Nonprofit Management Associa-
    tion, 57, 61, 64
Nonprofit Resource Institute, 64
North American Wildlife and
    Natural Resources Con-
    ference, 48
North American Wolf Society, 45
Northern Lights, 85
Northern Rockies Action Group,
    46-48, 51-52, 55-56

Occupational Safety and Health
    Administration, 74
Office of Education, U.S., 50, 74,
    76
Omnibus Budget Reconciliation
    Act, 76

Organizing. *See* Communications

Pennsylvania State University, 59
Perrine, Richard, 69
Philanthropy. *See* Funding
    sources, private philanthropic
Policy development, 22-23
    comparative need for, *9*
    effect of federal policy on, 4-5
    need for, by environmental
        groups, 39-40, *24, 25, 26*
    resources for training in, 85-86
    see also Research
"Preventing Burnout in the Public
    Interest Community"
    (article), 46-47
Programs, training. *See* Resources
Public Management Institute, 57
Public Services Materials Center,
    57
Publications, 57, *18, 20, 21*

Ramsay, Marsha, 74
Rastatter, Clem, 74
Research, 22-23
    comparative need for, *9*
    need for, by environmental
        groups, *24, 25, 26*
Resources
    Association of New Jersey
        Environmental Commissions,
        49, 55
    clearinghouse, 83-84
    community-organizing training
        centers, 64-66
    credentials for providers of,
        40-41
    development of new, 81-89
    environmental studies programs,
        66-73, 73, 86-87
    internships, 70-73, 87-88, *71*
    knowledge of, 46

Land Trust Exchange, 49-50, 55
League of Women Voters
    Education Fund, 53-55
linked to training needs, 83-84
management support organiza-
    tions, 61-64
for management training, 88-89
national, 49, 50, 52-55, 56-61
New England Environmental
    Network, 46, 50-51, 55, 76,
    82, 85
Northern Rockies Action
    Group, 46-48, 51-52, 55-56
PIRGs, 72-73
for policy training, 85-86
provided by environmental
    groups, 42
provided by nonenvironmental
    organizations, 56-73
publications, 57
regional, 48, 49, 50-52, 61-64
Sierra Club, 10, 19, 52-53, 55
traditional institutions, 56-60
trainers, 40-41, 84-85
for training, 45-78
universities, 59-60, 66-73, 86-87
see also Environmental groups;
    Institutions
Resource Directory for Funding
    and Managing Nonprofit
    Organizations, 57, 83
Resources and Strategies for Im-
    proving the Management of
    Nonprofit Organizations, 64
Retired Senior Volunteer Project
    (RSVP), 63
Robberson, Nancy, 55
Ronald Press, 57
Rutgers University, 75

Sierra Club, 10, 19, 52-53, 55
Skills. See Training needs
Solar Lobby, 65

SPIRES Service, 64
Stanford University, 59
Stone Foundation, 64
Support Center, The, 62, 63, 64

Taft Corporation, 57
Technical assistance. See Resources
Technical Assistance Center, 62
Technology, office. See Manage-
    ment, internal
Tennessee Environmental Council,
    48
Thacker, Sandra Gray, 45
Trainers. See Resources, trainers
Training, 57
Training and Development Jour-
    nal, 57
Training and Development
    Organizations Directory, 57
Training institutions. See
    Institutions
Training materials. See Resources
Training needs
    changes in, in 1980s, 3-5
    in communications, 17-22, 18,
        20, 21
    comparative importance of,
        39-42, 9
    in education, 17-22, 18, 20, 21
    effect of federal policy on, 4-5
    in fund-raising, 8-12, 9, 10, 11
    funding sources for, 74-78
    by individual skills, 113-118
    in internal management, 12-17,
        40, 13, 15, 16
    in membership recruitment,
        8-12, 9, 10, 11
    methodology for assessing, 5-6,
        93-96
    in policy development, 22-23,
        39-40, 24, 25, 26
    provided for, by environmental
        groups, 33-36, 42, 48-56, 30,
        32

questionnaire for assessing,
    101-111
ranking of, 23-33, 81-83, *27, 28,*
    29, 30, 31, 32, 34-35
in research, 22-23, *24, 25, 26*
and resource linkage, 83-84
resources for, 45-78
Training programs. *See* Resources
Training resources. *See* Resources
Tufts University, 50

UCLA, 68-69, 70
United Way, 60, 63
Urban Development Action Grant,
    76
Urban Environment Conference,
    65-66

Vermont, University of, 73
Virginia Forestry Association, 48
Volunteers. *See* Management,
    internal
Volunteer: National Center for
    Citizen Involvement, 60

Washington, University of, 45
Washington Wilderness Coalition,
    45
Weber, Isabelle, 54
Weyerhauser Foundation, 64
*Who's Who in Training and
    Development*, 58
Wildlife Management Institute, 48

Xerox, 77

Yale University, 23, 40, 70-72, 73,
    78
Youth Project, The, 62

The Authors

J. Clarence Davies, executive vice-president of The Conservation Foundation, is an authority on environmental research and public policy. He is the author of *Politics of Pollution* and *Neighborhood Groups and Urban Renewal* and coeditor of *Business and Environment: Toward Common Ground* (first edition).

Frances H. Irwin, a Conservation Foundation associate, specializes in hazardous waste and toxic substances control. She is coauthor of *Public Policy for Chemicals: National and International Issues* and other Foundation reports on toxic substances issues. She also has coordinated several citizen-training conferences.

Barbara K. Rodes is the Conservation Foundation's research librarian. She has served as a librarian for several nonprofit organizations and as education director for a citizens' environmental group in Pennsylvania concerned with strip-mining issues.